205 Thoughts from the Heart of a Man

205 Thoughts from the Heart of a Man

by Alan Alston Sr.

ReadersMagnet, LLC

Contents

"Time and Place for Everything"

There's a time to fight, I mean only in war,
but in all actuality what is it good for.
There's a time to reap and a time to sow.
Reap is what you get back
and sow is what you dish out.
Anytime and any place
it all seem to balance out.
Capital punishment has a place and a time.
It is written in scriptures an eye for an eye.
If God is to judge then how can I?
Place your self in a different scene.
The time is death and it's not a dream.
Its inevitable when your numbers called.
Who's to blame when you start to fall.
The flames are hot and if that's not all.
The worms never stop, through your body they crawl.
Heaven or Hell there's a time and a place.
You alone can pick the way that you seal your fate.
The time is judgment and the place is eternal.
There's either joy in Heaven or torment in an inferno.

2

"Shine"

Shine my young people shine.
Everything is going to be fine.
Always look up to the sky.
There is hope for you in my eyes.
Once I couldn't see the dilemma.
Now I know, because I remember.
There are lessons I've been
taught as a young lad.
In spite of the trouble there's
no need to be sad.
Perhaps one day you'll see.
How fun it is to be free.
So shine my young people, shine.
You are forever on my mind.
There's a seed that has been planted
from your day of birth.
It's up to you to make it work.
You've been called to be the light of the earth.
Just shine my young people shine.
The reason that I can be quoted,
was because I almost lost my shine.

I got confused, thinking the world was all mine.
Then I had to consider right from wrong.
I had no idea that my light was almost gone.
But I remembered to pray for a better way.
Please God don't take my light away.
Things worked out fine. I do intend to shine.
So now I'll pass it down, the power of the light.
Continue to do right and maintain a healthy change.
A world full of darkness is full of bad things.
Remember the seed that I told you
about close to the start.
Let this flow like water,
to grow love in your heart.
So shine my young people shine.

3

"Persecute"

Why?
Tell me is it okay to punish unjustly,
to speak with contempt or to lie just to discredit?
By not means is it okay.
There shouldn't be debate because the truth separates.
We have right or wrong, good or bad,
real or fake, love or hate.
Just because I claim Christianity there's no need to dis.
We all aim for a target but some of us miss.
I have only one target and the direction is up above.
Every time I hit the mark all I receive is love.
So I'll give it back because that's what I have to give.
Christ gave the same thing
but the world didn't want him to live.
Do you persecute when your neighbor does right?
Calling them hypocrites and your not living right.
Those that don't know why I follow
Jesus come up with their own conclusions.
Is this the reason we have persecution?
Is there a solution?

There certainly are some problems,
only love can help us solve them.
Any one can be a hypocrite.
The definition is counterfeit.
So why persecute on another
especially one of opposite color?
It really shouldn't matter what you are.
We should encourage and press
on if we want to go far.
My conclusion is to those with faith.
The end is near and the world will hate.
If you know the truth then it knows you.
There's no escape people will persecute.
They'll call you a lie and even make up
some but in the end you know you've won.
A loser talks about and makes up excuses
when he loses but a winner deals in facts
because the truth Is what he uses.

4

"Metaphors"

A metaphor is a figure of speech.
"Every life is unique."
"Don't talk when grown folk speak."
"Excuse me!"
"Life is so sweet."
See what I mean.
A metaphor is an everyday thing.
"It's hotter than hell."
"Time to hit the old dusty trail."
"You greedy pig."
"My goal is to get big, you dig."
"Cunning as a sniper."
I'm relaxed not hyper.
"I'm as busy as a beaver,
old school like the Cleavers."
"Beam me up Scottie."
"Like a hot toddy I'll warm up the body."
"You're a hottie so don't be snobby."
"Don't be snottie meat me in the lobby."
"I'm brown like Bobby and foxy like Brown."
You know it's all good, come on now.

"I'll raise the roof up like stilts."
"Keep you warm like a quilt."
"Yes, I'm yielding while defying the rules."
The truth are my tools.
"Grow up and plant your roots like a tree."
Bare fruit, sow your seed.
"Stay on point like a blade."
Open your blinds, don't draw the shades.
Let the light shine in.
"Why be funky like breaking wind?"
"Stubborn as a donkey."
Play to win. "Climb like a monkey."
Until the end.
"Open your ears and not your mouth."
Call before you come over to my house.
"If at first you don't succeed then try, try again."
"I'm a lover not a fighter,"
marking my territory like a Tiger.
"I am chief like the King."

"In the end the strong will last."
"The last will be first and the first will be last."
Quote these words they will come to pass.
"I've found the key to open the door
prompting myself to rise from the floor."

5

"Go"

Run a good race. Stay at your own pace.
You don't have to place.
Just as long as you finish with grace.
The future is ahead of you and your past is behind.
The hands of time, they don't have rewind.
Just go, you'll do fine.
Hey, I know.
I've been there too.
Feelings of rejection not knowing what to do.
Misunderstood but I knew that I could.
No one ever told me no one ever would.
For some reason I let others silence my dreams.
I thought running in a pack was the safest thing.
Ultimately I had to think,
a chain breaks at its weakest link.
My link, that had been cracked
was believing in the pack.
When in fact, I can watch my own back.
So I had to go!
In this condition you don't need recognition.
Stay at your mission. Realize your position.

Find out what's missing.
Your ability to achieve has been granted.
Hostility deceives, that life is slanted.
The finish is the truth and its <u>Enchanted.</u>
Delighted beyond measure is the correct definition.
Besides it is treasure, what a mission. So go.
You might stumble and trip.
Fall down, bust your lip. Get up!
Giving up isn't hip.
That's what happened to so many others.
They didn't get cut from the team.
Deception stole their dream.
You can't quit and that's the truth.
You have to finish the race. It's up to you.
If you run in the truth then you can't loose.
<u>JUST GO!</u>

6

"Faith"

It is defined as belief,
trust and confidence.
Which is evidence of something hoped for.
It is being sure for what is hoped
and certain of what we do not see.
Belief is to have faith, agreeing
to the mind, accepting as true.
Which is trust, called reliance.
That is the act of relying.
So when we rely on trust
we can rest with confidence.
This is assurance meaning secure
confidence or insurance.
So Faith is not hope.
It is firm confirmation of what is.
Meaning to be.

7

"Save Me"

Save me from the pain.
Shelter me from the rain.
Rescue me I need help.
Tell me who is able
to save me from myself?
I call out with my silence.
At times I call out using violence.
Please save me, I'm in distress.
Where is my savior
when I waddle in my mess.
I pray to be cleansed,
I long to be blessed.
My life is sinking and time is getting short.
Will I be able to rise without support?
Will I find justice if I can't afford a lawyer in court?
I refuse to go down without a fight.
I'll mustard up all of my faith using all of my might.
I'm told to hold on,
stay strong but the grave won't let me be.
Using my faith I will wait until some one, Saves me.

8

"Laughter"

The sound of laughing when we are merry.
Laughter can chase away emotions,
like the feeling we get if something is scary.
It's a bubbling form of jay that explodes
when things are funny.
We laugh at jokes executed properly can
be hilarious for a period of time.
There's even laughter when watching a mime.
These explosion of humor make us laugh until we cry.
Tears of joy flowing from our eyes.
Cheerfulness at this point has a degree of healing.
It's good therapy no matter what we are feeling.
Laughter is optimistic, it brings hope.
A good laugh could help us cope.
With an ordeal that leaves us in a mess.
Laughter is good for relieving all types of stress.

"Tenderness"

Sweetness, gentle, delicate and tame.
The essence of a flower tenderness is you name.
Fleeting your not when you walk.
Subtle you speak when you talk.
Just like art that's in a frame.
Submissive are your needs modest with out shame.
Light as a feather, tender is your touch.
More valuable than a jewel
that makes you worth so much.
Elegance is your companion
which follows you where ever you go.
Harmonious and soft, so very unique.
Tenderness you are tenderness you will be.

10

"Praise"

When I lift my heart up to the sky,
I'm caught up in a daze.
I set my mind on you and I am amazed.
It brings me joy every time I give you the praise.
I am set free, no loner feeling like a rat in a maze.
In spite of the world that surrounds me.
In a large crowd I can still bow down on my knee.
You are my laughter in times of grief.
You are my joy when I need relief.
In times of trouble,
I still know that you are real.
You never charge me.
With you I have no bill.
How do I repay you for all that you have done?
I've done some bad things,
but you remember none.
To you I give the praise.
For you are the one.

11

"Hurry"

Time is running out.
The clock is ticking.
Come quick.
Are you weighed down,
like packing a ton of bricks?
Lighten your load,
you're moving to slow.
Its time to go. Let's hit the road.
Hop to it like a toad.
Don't be late, it might not wait.
What's the rush?
You might miss the bus.
Do you have the time?
It's going to be fine.
I'll just wait until tomorrow.
Don't put it off you might be sorrow.
No indeed.
Then check your speed.
What does is read?
It says take heed.

What does it mean?
This is not a dream.
It means the end.
Oh no! Not that again!
If the end is scary then I suggest you hurry.

12

"You Are"

You are happiness in the light of day.
You are sunshine when the skies are gray.
You are mine no matter what.
You are no if, ands or buts.
You are travel and I want to go there.
You belong to me and I'm willing to share.
You are not selfish when it comes to my needs.
You are a rose in a garden full of weeds.
You are plenty and I can't get enough.
You are that good stuff.
You are air that I breathe in my lungs.
For you I will share, for you are the one.
You are my strength when I feel weak.
There is only one of you, you are unique.
I will always think about you, seven days a week.
You are the one.
You are for me.

13

"Clay"

You are the potter I am the clay.
I'm your work of art; you made me this way.
I was shaped to be something,
I know not yet what.
Yes, I'm the vessel of your will. If you fill
me up then of course I will spill.
I can't contain the wisdom of my creator.
The clay is the former the creation comes later.
If I could create myself to be what I want
then I wouldn't need you but I'll never say I don't.
You thought about me and then made me one day.
You are the potter I am the clay.

14

"Power"

Presuming, Only, Warriors, Earn, Reverence
Which is respect!
Bring it direct! So recollect.
The command has been warranted this very hour.
Displays of forwardness using all power.
Strength to endure,
perseverance to insure my existence.
Unshaken so I'll withstand any weapon
devised by entity or man.
There are other entities greater than me.
I can do what I am called to be.
My way has passage to walk through and I will fight.
Capable to act, able to use my might.
Awesome I was born, devastating I will be!
I've been granted authority, destine to be free.
A man who has power, a man I will be!

15

"Now"

It is time to act.
Why hold back?
When in fact.
You know the exact.
At this present time you should know what to do.
Who deceives you?
Stand your ground.
The time is now!
Don't wait until later,
now is much greater.
Having goals are fine but prioritizing
will make our Paths straight.
Act right now you don't have to wait.
You may have to let to of the old but be bold.
Sad days might have to occur
and you often wonder, "How?"
Wait until those days come or prepare for them, " Now."

16

"Hedge"

A hedge is before me, behind and on my sides.
The hedge around me is there, but it is not to hide.
I am surrounded by a hedge for protection.
My hedge is placed to restrain any imperfections.
A hedge can be a fence to guard us
from what we are up against.
Intruder come to attack but a hedge
keeps my enemies back.
A hedge is not trendy a hedge defends me.
A hedge has a place; my hedge grows by grace.
If deceivers choose to enter my favor
trying to use a wedge.
There are boundaries that surround me,
so I'll let wisdom be my hedge.

17

"Rich"

Being rich can teach some lessons.
Rich is defined as having abundant possessions.
Rich can be wealthy.
To me rich, is to remain healthy.
Some see rich for what it's worth.
I see rich for potential hurt.
Rich is having exactly what we need.
Having much more of that, can manifest greed.
Rich is knowing who we are; rich is not a fancy car.
Rich is capable to understand,
rich is not five thousand grand.
Rich is caring for other folk.
What would a rich person do,
if they suddenly went broke?
I'm not trying to burst your bubble.
Rich is having friends in a time of trouble.
Rich is plenty but I have much more.
I have my liberty and it's insured.
Rich has a price, like a pair of new gloves.
Rich can be nice if we are rich with love.

"Feelings"

Like a child with a favorite toy.
I favor the feelings of joy.
Feelings of shame hurt worst than feeling of pain.
Feelings of sadness are madness compared to gladness.
Attraction is a feeling that can be mixed with passion.
I have feelings of pressure when I need compassion.
I have a feeling of safety to say the least,
when I have feelings, the feeling of peace.
My feeling of belief is directed up above
because I know the feeling of the one true love.
The feeling of humility can bring healing.
The reason I know this is because I am someone.
Someone with feelings.

19

"Vision"

Visions might seem sometimes extreme.
I am a visionary one who has dreams.
Visions my come and visions my go.
Sometimes they are not sometimes they are so.
Close your eyes and vision your youth.
Can you see the vision, the visions of truth?
Visions of old are the past that was told.
If it is so then that vision is gold.
Visions are seen conscious or in a dream.
King saw a vision, King has a dream.

20

"Structure"

It's the creativity of a plan or ideal thought of.
There first must be an understanding of structure.
An organization of the proceeding.
Established the boundaries effectively for a purpose.
A structure is superficial meaning on the surface.
Before I knew purpose I had to be built.
Not with poles or stilts, but a make up of guilt.
We see the surface of a person for appeal.
The inner makes our exterior feel.
Which was thought of for effectiveness,
so that our hearts can be organized.
The structure of a person has just been recognized.
So that means, "I have been built in a man-
ner complementing a plan. There for the inner
makes the outer structure of a man.

21

"Verily"

Really and truly I believe.
It truly is a privilege.
I really am blessed.
Life verily gives us a test.
Can it really be a quest?
Verily, verily what is next.
Honestly, I truly didn't know.
Is it really so?
Truly it must be.
Of course, there really and truly is no other explanation.
Surely there is one?
Certainly.
How do you truly know?
I really and truly have faith.
That's it! What?
The truth. Verily.

22

"Join Me?"

Come on lets walk together.
Let's talk together.
Join me, we can do whatever.
Hey friend, why do you sit alone?
I will invite you into my home.
Join me there's no need to be afraid.
We'll stand in the light together, away from the shade.
Join me for something to eat.
Don't worry it's my treat.
It doesn't matter if you're a stranger of a friend.
You're invited. just take my hand.
Welcome; come on in from the cold.
Why do I do so?
I'm just doing what I've been told.
Love thy neighbor as thy self.
Ask a favor, I'll try to help.
Well, I have others to ask you see.
I'm on a mission but first will you, join me?

23

"Not that Simple"

We say that we will but we won't.
I want us to try but we don't.
Why do we say sorry, when we get caught?
Like originally it wasn't our fought.
Can I quit; my body is a temple?
It's more complex then that it's not that simple.
Giving gifts on Christmas is traditional.
We say, I love you, is it unconditional?
You want to stay together but you cheated.
How do I know if it will be repeated?
I won't do it anymore, are your words.
Should I forgive you or is it up surd?
It's just not that simple. This is difficult to do.
For you too?
I don't understand, please explain.
Circumstances are strange. They might change.
It really doesn't have to be the same.
That's a shame, why?
It's not that simple.

24

"Pressure"

I am weighed down on every side.
So much pressure I just want to hide.
Listen up, I can't take much more.
Things are tightening up, can I endure?
There is pressures everyday.
I have to watch the things I say.
I feel pressure in work or play.
Am I going the right way?
There is pressure to learn, pressure to earn,
pressure to yearn and pressure to concern.
When we are young we're pressured by our peers.
Then we get old we are pressured by the golden years.
A facial expression marks the pressure of fear.
There are pressures to be pure.
Disease pressures a cure.
I am trying to stay free.
I am pressure just being me.
Pressure can increase but when there is pressure,
there are needs of release.
So pressure temporarily has to cease
allowing wisdom to increase.

25

"Grow"

The day you're conceived, you are as small as a seed.
Indeed, you are so, but not yet able to feel the wind blow.
In the process you are nurtured for a life.
If your taken well care of then strong
roots will hold you upright.
The wind blows, the rain comes,
it snows and you're young.
You sprout up to reach the light destine to grow bold.
Everything that has breath has to grow old.
You adapt to your surroundings
and to the things you know.
Every creature is created even
some of them have a foe.
Be what you are supposed to be
and if you're not then you can.
Live out you're existence unto your life span.
The foe of life is death it truly is so.
Remember and you will know that the mind
can kill the body if it does not grow.

"To Arms"

Be alert!
Something's lurking to see you hurt.
You're being accused, to arms don't be used.
Sound the alarm, charm can abuse.
You're a target and you are insight.
Stand firm be prepared for a fight.
It is known where you are headed.
Eyes linger all around, only to discredit.
Stand your ground, only where the righteous has treaded.
There is anger because you know the way.
To arms every single day.
Your protection comes with faith.
Confidence is in the wait.
You're like a boat that battles a raging storm
but hope is like a paddle there will be no harm.
I say prepare yourself. say take care of yourself.
To Arms!

27

"Exempt"

One that obeys the law is exempt from jail.
Christians faithfully believe that they are exempt from hell.
The wise is exempt from being called a fool
because the wise remembers that wisdom's a tool.
We are privilege to be free, exempt from slavery.
Only if we submit to authority daily.
There are no exceptions to a rule.
Compromise leaks stubbornness as if in a mule.
Being freed from danger is not in the plan.
You will experience some, every woman, girl, boy and man.
Judge not by the standards of a man, if you can.
We are obligated to do well for our community.
Together we stand strong, only in unity.
We all are models there is no immunity.
And there's no denial, there will be trials, so make an attempt.
We will be tested on righteousness, no one's exempt.

28

"Watch"

Open your eyes and look.
See what is opposing you.
The opposition is there to defeat.
Do not retreat! Watch!
Use what you are given to recognize the enemy.
Which should be discernment.
Understanding the tactics used one
can eliminate a possible collision.
The signs are obviously hidden.
Keep watch, you have been warned.
Yes, you should be alarmed.
The mind is a lighthouse to the body,
so make your next move just
as soon as you're approached.
Having a conscience tells yourself
that you've been coached.
There might be an attack from the blind side.
Watch! Stay on guard because everyday
a chance to get you will be made.
Stay awake do not slumber or sleep.
The enemy wants you to feel weak.

Exercise your strength, train to endure,
always be sure of that which flows in you are pure.
It's not that complex.
Just be ready for whatever's next, so watch!

29

"I Messed Up"

That's what I did.
I felt so ashamed I could have hid.
I realized my mistake.
Is your forgiveness all that it would take?
Please forgive me.
I'm in a rut.
I feel this way because I messed up.
I should have listened and done it your way.
Next time I will do exactly what you say.
Will there be a next time, another chance?
If so I'll be fine because I will advance.
I was given directions as easy as adding water to a cup.
If I had followed then I wouldn't have messed up.
Disobedience had me stalling.
So I did it my way falling.
Now I have to make amends for my actions.
The proper amount of discipline demands satisfaction.
I understand that it has to be tuff.
Please forgive me, I hope that will be enough?
You are my father and I am your pup.
You are right, I messed up.

30

"Three Wishes"

If I had three wishes and they would all come true.
My first wish would be, first to get to know you.
If I had three wishes and they all would come true.
My second wish would be, to always please you.
If I had three wishes and all three did come true.
My third and final wish would be to always love you.
I have only three wishes and now you know.
That's the way that I feel, so let my wishes be so.

31

"Doing Fine"

You're doing fine, try not to worry so much.
You're doing fine.
Why depend on luck?
Luck is never a guarantee
because bad luck is also there,
don't you agree?
You're doing fine.
Just keep on trying.
You're doing fine.
No I'm not lying.
Remember those times that you thought were all bad.
They made you depressed, they made you sad.
Things started to work out,
and then someone made you mad.
You remembered that there's a way and now you are glad.
Consider what I say, "It's only for a time."
Don't forget about today.
You are doing fine.
You're doing fine, I know because I do.
You're doing fine because I doubt just like you.

You're doing fine.
I know that you have stress.
That's the way it is, you'll do fine its only a test.
I have already considered all of your needs;
you will be fine, You will indeed.

32

"Hate"

I hate the way I fornicate.
I hate to have to wait for the breaks that a wait my fait.
I hate that people are lost for what it costs to be the boss.
Without knowing the inner structure of our existence.
We think that we know too much,
be still for awhile, be quiet you need to listen.
I hate to miss the point if I need it.
Can one say that it will be repeated?
In times of trouble who will run or stand firm.
Yes, I am concerned.
That's why I hate to see people not on good terms.
I hate the fact that I'm not perfect.
All my faults are on the surface.
I hate that pain will come.
Will I persevere, or will I run?
I hate the fact that I don't always obey.
I thought that I've learned my lessons back in the day.
Apparently not but I didn't miss the point,
that cuts like a knife.
That's why I changing because I hate my old life.

33

"Thank You"

In these word that I (you) now read.
They are for you, for you to receive.
It's out of love that I express the way I feel.
Every single line truly is for real.
I know that you will accept my thanks.
There's appreciated interest, like money in the bank.
This is overwhelming support, for little old me.
I must confess it's like honey to a bee.
I've greatly been tested while walking in my shoes.
I understand the concept of obeying the rules.
It brings pleasure to my heart, when I know that you approve.
That's why I took out this time to re-sight (write),
Thank You.

34

"Joy"

Shear delight, I give my word as a plight.
To honor joy, yeah that's right.
It truly excites one's appetite.
A solemn promise of bliss.
Happiness that's wished.
Expectation, like a first kiss.
Rejoice in the pleasure that is caused by goodness.
Be encouraged because joy brings cheerfulness.
Smiles are seen, laughter is heard.
There's no better feeling.
I've given you my word.
Nothing can compare to the feeling of joy.
There's no shame in it, no need to be coy.
Joy can triumph victoriously over grief.
Gladness not sorrow, "Oh what a relief."
It can't be explained if you know what I mean.
Just try to obtain this wonderful theme.
"Joy"

35

"Savor"

Enjoy every minute of the day and savor what you have not.
If it's taken away then you might not have another shot.
So savor what you've got.
Cherish love if you understand the meaning of devotion.
Savor the idea that it's broader than the ocean.
Dedication can be honor with praise.
Let go of the past you will be amazed.
Just savor the present and delight in what's ahead.
Do not decide on either or but choose both instead.
Be particular about what's best for you.
Savor the decision, your will to choose.
Open up to new ideas and partake into fresh thoughts.
Stay away from negativity and pointing out one's faults.
Watch what you savor.
Love your neighbor.
You will be granted favor.
For all good behavior.

36

"If and Then"

If I could then I would always be good.
If I knew my problems then I could try to solve them.
If it wasn't for taste then I wouldn't know the flavor.
If I stay on my best behavior then I will be granted favor?
If I didn't try then how would I know that I can.
If it weren't any rules then how could justice stand?
If I didn't have lungs then how can I take a breath?
If it weren't for life then there wouldn't be death.
If we didn't have hope then it would be hard to cope.
If there were no justice then we would have no mercy.
If times were always great then they wouldn't seem odd.
If it wasn't for faith then I wouldn't believe in God.
Find out the truth and flee from sin.
If today you die what would happen then?

37

"I was Created"

I was created; I didn't evolve from a monkey.
Theory says so but it's ass as a donkey.
I am too complex to have just come about.
My existence was planned,
in my heart there is no doubt.
I was created.
I don't speak scientifically
because science was created by a man.
Science rules out the Godhead
because science doesn't understand.
What is natural is not man made.
So why the shade?
I was created.
What I was taught in school
was very different from church.
It was up to me to receive some spiritual worth.
People threw in some curves and believe me they hurt.
Sending mixed signals eliminating Christ birth.
"Who should we believe?"
Well it's all up to you and your faith.
It is not to be debated. I know with whom I stand.
"I was created."

38

"Everyone has Trouble"

Don't think that for one minute you're in this alone.
One dog does not chew on every bone.
No matter how delightful others may seem.
Everyone has trouble.
Which is the theme.
Even the peaceful struggle when there is war.
The rich are broken when they get poor.
The poor are pressed when they can't buy bread.
Leaders are threatened when no one follows what is said.
So don't look at others as if they're in a bubble.
No life is perfect. "Everyone has Trouble."
Loneliness, stress, disease and mentally depressed
all have people caught up in a mess.
Having the lack of with no love.
There are also habitual cravings for drugs.
People are stricken with alcoholism and abuse,
missing parents without excuse.
Disrespectful children, unfaithful needs,
financial discomfort and suicidal pleas.
Look around, you're not the only one.

Don't be down while others are having fun.
Rejoice with your neighbor
and sympathize when there's pain.
A friend shares an umbrella when two walk in the rain.

39

"Take It"

There are a lot of things in this world
that are of no value to me.
Only the valuable things that are apart
of my heart came for free.
I know love. I can't fake it.
Money can't buy it and no one can take it.
Yes, I will share it. The price is free.
If you get near it then you will agree.
If you take it then it's not yours.
If I give it freely then it's worth much more.
Did you know there are consequences to actions?
If I choose to take things, it might bring me shame.
If I decide to wait then I can enjoy the change.
I'll stay on guard to avoid being shamed.
I had taken a path that wasn't on the map.
Then I got lost, was it only a trap?
I realized the dilemma; there was a need.
If it's one thing I should have took
then it should have been heed.
Oh, I just realized. It has always been free.

40

"Good Is"

Good is what good does.
All good deeds don't come from love.
Give because it's good.
Share because you should.
Be aware of what good is and what good is not.
Like a smiling stare may be a plot.
Watch because good is what good does.
Offer your assistance when there is needed help.
Paying attention is good for one's self.
I will walk the distance for a friend.
I can even listen until the end.
Some ways are very distinct.
The truth is sweet but a lie does stink.
Like a bee will buzz.
Good is what good does.
Good is laughter, which brings us joy.
Good is a baby girl or boy.
Good is pleasant which is unique.
Good is subtle, humble and meek.
Good is not jealous, but good is zealous.
Eager to do exactly what it planned.
Good is how we should be. Understand!

"Jesus"

What is it about that name?
You are known for the sacrifice.
Which wasn't done for fame.
It was done for redemption to save all souls.
Only those who believe are the ones who truly know.
Jesus, I was taught that you are the Father.
I've been taught you are the Son.
I was prompt in receiving your spirit.
I believe the three are really one.
You are life itself.
The very breath of my existence.
In my life I have to obey.
So I guess I'll handle my business.
Jesus, you are the word and the word stands for truth.
I'm glad that you showed my mother
because she taught me in my youth.
Now I can teach my kids unconditional love.
That only comes from Jesus. The only Jesus above.

42

"Purpose"

Every living creature has a purpose.
Up above, underneath and on the surface.
Each person was designed to do a task.
There use to be a time when I would walk
around aimlessly as if I wore a mask.
Obstacles cloud our vision making us blind.
Until we repent greatly renewing one's mind.
It's exciting to chase away old life threats.
I have a purpose; there are no regrets.
Identity tries to haunt us.
Temptations try to taunt us.
Evil wants to flaunt us but Jesus really wants us.
According to faith I see evidence that leaves a trace.
Written on every face.
We all receive Grace.
Walk after your crawl.
Get up when you fall.
Just start when you stall.
Live for a cause.
Closed minded is not worth it.
Our lives have a purpose.

43

"Fair Weather"

Times get tough; days still won't remain the same.
Spite the obstacles our faith still remains.
When the skies are cloudy it could potentially rain.
Holding on to persevere the days will get better.
No need to complain there will come fair weather.
Be strong for more than one reason.
Does the sun shine during all four seasons?
It has been said, "Times do get tough."
Believe fair weather is coming, I can't proclaim it enough!
Have patience whether sunshine or a storm.
Birth was a task that day we were born.
Pain will pass so don't be torn.
No need to be spiteful and no need to mourn.
Just try to be delightful in the mist of your storm.
The sun makes it better to give us fair weather.
Anticipate duress we all will feel stressed.
Trying to wonder what happens next?
Isn't life only a test?
Of course it's perplexed.
There are levels of difficulty but still do your best.
Our lives are knitted right as if though a sweater.
So try not to unravel there will be fair weather.

44

"Greetings"

Come on in.
"What can I do for you?"
You say that you need a friend, well that may be true.
Tell me what would you like to say?
I've been there for you everyday.
Why did you wait until there was trouble?
If you'd called sooner
then I would have been there on the double.
The truth is really not that bad.
Why are you shedding tears?
Is it because you are glad?
Well, that's good to hear because you appeared very sad.
Go ahead ask me a favor.
Whatever it is I won't get mad.
You want things to be peaceful.
I think I can do that.
I've already conquered evil.
Certainly, I've got your back.
Why am I so kind?
It's because I know your pain.
The world didn't like me, it will do you the same.

Especially since you made this choice.
You've asked for a change.
Now go live a life of peace my friend.
But don't forget our meeting.
Tell a couple of your friends some-
times and I'll extend my greetings.

45

"Double Edge Sword"

To the body and mind from the power of the word.
Now you have heard.
Words which are far from absurd.
The truth is the Word.
Consider these words.
The sword when slung can slice in two.
The knowledge of it can separate the wise from a fool.
The thrust from a deadly blow penetrates to the bone.
Eradicating a lie the truth holds it's own.
When the enemy approaches with his vicious horde.
Remember that you alone can slay ten thousand
with the double edge sword.
To the body and mind from the power of the Lord.
Consider these words it is foolishness to disregard.
Gods' wrath will conquer over its' foes that oppose.
What has been told from the days of old.
The double edge sword will convict whether poor or rich.
When it strikes it splits.
It allows the wise man to have confirmation
and the foolish man will quiver.
The word of God and the fear of it
should make you shiver.

46

"So Be It"

There are things in this world that I can't change.
Un-explainable events that are considered strange.
I walk through this world sensitive to the needs of all people.
Looking forward to the day that good conquers evil.
Truly this is the way to go.
Let your yes be yes and your no be no.
When the storm comes a river flows swift.
Being forgiven for wrong is such a wonderful gift.
Good fruit comes from a good tree.
Knowledge is understood as the key.
Why would a blind man try to lead?
Only because he knows that his followers can't possibly see.
Is this why so many are lead astray?
Seek the right path there's only one true way.
Orchestrate your life and I'll do mine.
Leave the past behind it's suspended in time.
Peace is on our wish list.
If we work together then we can get through this.
Deal with today and its' struggles, be strong.
Don't worry about tomorrow it has troubles of its' own.

47

"Fully Filled"

Everyday I feel pleasure even though there are trials.
I am blessed.
There are mountains of joy heaped before me.
There are springs of love flowing around me.
There is also goodness above me.
As well as a foundation of stability beneath me.
If these blessings were not so could one survive?
Definitely one could try.
Since I've accepted this could I be deprived?
No, of course not the truth is alive.
From there to here could be a long distance.
From scared to fear isn't part of my existence.
Live to plant, plant to harvest. Labor regardless.
I was found because I was lost.
Liberty has a cost.
The reason I searched was to find.
Now, I have mine.
Opened doors are a token.
I knocked and they were opened.
For the truth there will always be an urge.
Why? Because in my youth I asked to be purged.

48

"Solitude"

Alone inside of my mothers womb.
Kicking and squirming trying to make room.
This is the way it feels when liberty
has been striped with no cause.
Lonely, cold days are cloudy
as if surrounded by fog.
Sustained by faith I press on.
Delivered by Grace, I'll hold on.
Recklessly I'll search for a place not so isolated.
Separated I am that day it was stated.
A boy was created.
Destined to be a man who is hated.
Division took place with genuine
emotions written upon my face.
I must stand-alone in a lonely place.
Trapped in this world full of moral decay.
A physical death is the only way.
We will one day be released from pain and strife.
Solitude can be a lonely life.
The day we're conceived is when it first begins.
The last breath I take is when all my pain will end.
Glory is to God because I'll be with him again.
Never alone, Amen.

49

"I Wonder"

There are a lot of thoughts that have crossed my mind.
There are a lot of unanswered questions and not enough time.
If I had the answers then I could make it thunder.
But I'm not God; I am a man, so I wonder.
I wonder about my Creator.
I wonder about my problems now and find the answer later.
I wonder how to get it right.
I wonder about that issue everyday and every night.
I wonder about those in need.
I wonder if I'm a flower or a weed?
I wonder if I don't or do I care?
I wonder if I won't or will I share?
Yes, I wonder and I guess it's not that strange.
There is a broader way of wondering so I wonder the range.
I wonder.

50

"Table Scraps"

Rectangle in shape with four legs.
Underneath are people who are fragile as eggs.
Our eyes are fixed on what lies ahead.
Anticipating the wait excited to receive our daily bread.
The table is set with all of its' trimmings.
We all get fed because the truth is winning.
The world is corrupt but prophesy tell us that we've won.
The Host of the banquet says that its' not yet done.
Something is cooking and a lot of folks can't smell the flavor.
It's the aroma of the bread of life,
which is referred to as the Savior.
From patience to perseverance, intercession for insurance these
are blessings in the form of table scraps.
One day we'll dine at the table, maybe, perhaps?
Table scraps are not a disgrace.
In no way please don't get me wrong.
They are Heavenly forms of blessings to
feed us for the rest of our life long.

51

"Tears"

A cry for delight.
It's from the joy of our lives over the years.
Happiness can bring tears.
Emotions erupt forming water in our eyes.
Instant therapy relieves us from pressure when one cries.
Everyone has issues, everyone has fears.
You're not alone because everyone sheds tears.
Tears are the evidence when the truth has been felt.
Humility is what I've been dealt.
On my knees I have knelt.
Feel the plight it is designed to open your ear.
It feels good to cry apart from our feelings that brings fear.
Suppression is not recommended as a good notion.
Tears are essential when one expresses devotion.
I've considered my words so be strong because the time is near.
For those who know will one day shed no more tears.

52

"Is This Real"

Is there an explanation for what I feel?
It has to be, this is real.
I talk to you and you listen.
You smile and it glistens.
When you speak you have my attention.
I feel something for you so this I must mention.
I don't want to mess this relationship up.
I know that you where sent to me
but I don't know for what.
Our love overflows like pouring too much in a cup.
This is so heavenly I can't agree that it's luck.
I'll open up my heart to you and to your heart I appeal.
We can make love come true.
We can keep this real.
Please care for my life like
I'm the only man on this planet.
Assure me that you will try
and not take me for granted.
Lets' pray on our steps,
so on our knees we shall kneel.
The answer will be on our hearts then
we will know that this is real.

53

"Understanding"

Knowing is understanding
and understanding is discernment.
I understand because it was meant.
It is said that a man and a dog
do some similar things.
But a man doesn't walk on all four
and a dog doesn't have a human's brain.
Some people are destine to try and improve life.
While others don't know that their always causing strife.
A person that's fruitful means they're a producer.
There's encouragement for us all to grow,
it determines our future.
It is understanding who we are
that puts us in a category.
The clues are ever present the truth tells the story.
What is truth to those that don't know?
There truly is one but all will not know.
There are choices to make and there's a direction?
Quit naturally there is and it points to perfection.
I said a mouthful, which took a small amount of planning.
Did I get my point across, the answer is understanding.

54

"Crowed Room"

Sitting alone in a room full of strangers.
Some live in safety while others live in dangers.
Not knowing what's on everyone's mind.
We live different lifestyles we're on different times.
There are open and closed doors that lead to many directions.
Pathways that have taught each of us lessons.
If the people in this crowed room could see into my life
then they would understand that this man has insight.
I sit back to observe the look on people's faces.
When this room is empty we will all be in different places.
So until then I'll slide over to make a little room.
My time spent here will be gone real soon.
If you ever see me again and I'm smiling,
singing a happy tune.
Remember the smile I had it was the
same in this crowed room.

55

"I Do"

I understand your pain when I talk to you.
I can relate to the problems that bother you.
I know that you get scared, so do I.
I know that this feels weird but we must try.
Be sensitive to my feelings and I'll be sensitive to yours.
Lets' do our best and open our hearts like doors.
If I put my guards down then you put down yours.
I'll make you a happy women this I know for sure.
I know that we've tried to do this before sometime in the past.
But if you decide to be my wife I promise it'll be the last.
I am not trying to confuse you then lose you
and cause both of us pain.
All I want is to bring us sunshine
after all those years of rain.
Do what you feel but follow your heart, which is true.
So if you ever want me the same then
I am prepared to say, I do.

56

"Overcome"

Times do get tuff but we're not helpless as if we're in a rut.
Exercise the authority that shows you superiority.
Mark off your territory.
To overcome is the priority.
Real is the opposite of fake.
Just as fear opposes faith.
Real is to be victorious over.
Its' meaning is to overcome.
Fake is to unresistingly yield or succumb.
Consider this, if you yield to fear
then how can you overcome?
To master faith, means that you've already won.
Believe in yourself especially in times of trouble.
The rain will stop and then joy will double.
We are not to take unnecessary chances.
Winning is to get the better of.
The finish is to overcome opposing circumstances.

57

"Change"

It is said that change is good.
Either you won't or you would.
Let it be understood change is for the good.
Certainly we should!
Just go back and reflect on my reasons.
Change can come in the form of four seasons.
Day changes to night and night into day.
A child changes to an adult and work can change into play.
So we must realize and always prepare.
Nothing stays the same, change will occur.
A caterpillar will change and then one day it will fly.
We can spread our wing from our cocoon if we try.
Take flight and understand one thing.
Nothing ever stays the same.
Like milk can be changed into butter.
Or one change can lead to another.
So can we eliminate the pain only if
we give ourselves unto change?

58

"Fade"

Everything that is not eternal away it will fade.
The sun passes by a tree giving us temporary shade.
As time goes on it will set ending our day.
Then comes the moon so that night can have its' way.
All things work together for good complimenting each other.
Renewal gives strength back to an object if it lost its' color.
Seal up your heart from evil so that you will not perish.
Keep it open to fruitful ideas
so that the truth can be cherished.
The grass will wither and the wind will blow.
Life will pass so that the spirit can go.
Bones can become brittle and muscles can lose strength.
The heart can love forever but the
beat becomes indistinct.
Remember those days when we where young
although they come and went.
These words are to keep you refreshed
because blessings are heaven sent.
Be blessed to know that love is the one thing
that isn't made.
If we work together then it can never fade.

59

"Security"

I'll open up my arms to you,
locking you in my embrace.
I'll comfort you when you need me
and wipe the tears from your face.
Feel free to call me anytime basically that means,
be confident.
If you don't understand
what I mean then security is what I meant.
There really is a guarantee so please don't despair.
Locked away in my heart is love that I will share.
I'll protect you from the things
of this world so there's no need to fear.
We've all expected so much better from
someone we thought was dear.
The stakes are high but love flows deep
which is my only weapon.
Because of the feelings
I have is the reason for my protection.
I'll lend you a hand if you shall fall and we can walk in unity.
I have a hunger to spread my love,
for this there is no immunity.

You're safe with me.
So can't you see.
You are very dear to me.
Just trust in me.
Then we will see.
Where there is trust there is, security.

60

"Decisions, Decisions"

Choices are inevitable this is something we all must face.
Examine your limitations before there is disgrace.
Indecisive decisions all of the time means
that the answer is kind of shady.
Confused in your thinking,
sometimes your direction will be very hazy.
Be definite when you make
a choice decisions have to be made.
If you make the wrong one
the consequences have to be paid.
Right or wrong whatever
the choice you have to make a decision.
Accidents do occur but mistakes cause collisions.
There's either or and neither nor.
When you decide you have to be sure.
If you can't make up your mind then don't leave it alone.
Some decisions that are made may not be our own.
Your fate is in your own hand whatever you decide.
Some things we can't take back and some of us try.
Decisions, decisions I wonder why?

61

"It's Catchy"

We could not run from it when we
were exposed to the truth.
Some time ago back when we were in our youth.
It was as if we had no say in the matter.
Our destiny was about to unfold
or our life was about to shatter.
It was hard to understand
why we feel different in our choice.
Are we robbed of our liberty?
Do we still have a voice?
Does change have to be accepted?
Now that we have caught it we could be rejected.
Be not fearful of something we can not control.
We have been chosen so we must assume our role.
There is a feeling that lies in us deep within.
Protection from death waging war against sin.
We still feel great which is joy to say the least.
Misunderstood because we live a life of peace.
Don't worry when the sun is covered and the fog is patchy.
It has already rubbed off because when
you have trust then love is catchy.

 ALAN ALSTON SR.

62

"Vicissitude"

Life changes are often strange especially what it might bring.
A lot of people get divorced while others covet the ring.
Commitment plays a significant part in vicissitudes.
Reciprocating events may spark many attitudes.
Horizontal thinking makes everything flat.
If there is a vertical inclination
then that is where we get the facts.
Highs and lows distinguish the difference in dreams.
Joyful people rejoice at life
while bitterness exposes silent screams.
We see expressions written upon each others face.
I look around me and wonder who knows a peaceful place.
It's sometimes involuntary what's going to happen next.
I don't believe in superstition
and it definitely rules out a hex.
Life is not for us to give or to take.
Be creative and learn from all mistakes.
"If it aint one thing then it is another."
"Oh brother!"
One of the ups and downs of life is called vicissitude.
One reason for the mess or blessed success is attitude.

63

"Today"

The moment I opened up my eyes
I just knew that I was loved by you today.
I'm confident that it's love
because last night for you I did pray.
When we talk our conversation
is laced with hope saturated with love.
You are strong yet you are soft as a dove.
I want to know if you have plans for today.
Let's come together so that we can be on our way.
It doesn't matter to me where we are going
just as long as you are there.
I'm always this serious, of course I really care.
My feelings are the same as yesterday.
That's the very reason I can say that I love you today.
You comfort me when there's pain
and celebrate with me when there is joy.
This makes me feel like a child with a favorite toy.
We work together as if you're the missing piece of the puzzle.
I confess you to be mine
so my mouth will never wear a muzzle.
Yes, this is real and not for play.
I knew it wasn't a dream the moment
that I woke up today.

64

"Gain"

It is not possible to lose and to gain at the same time.
Your either on the right or the left side of the line.
Knowledge can be acquired even if we are not eager to learn.
If you miss the point that's why I've showed concern.
Keeping up with the Jones is cut and cry.
I can see much better since the plank is out of my eye.
Observation recognizes that some events cause pain.
Be different from the norm being a copy cat is not a gain.
Selfishness is a curse so practice some self control.
Plan to the extent but always strive for the goal.
Can we hear thunder? See the clouds and feel the rain.
This means that the day is gloomy
and the night is the same.
Understand that in life there will be pain.
The storm is going to pass just wait for the change.
The sun will shine so that blessings, will be the gain.

65

"No Matter What"

It will always be understood that we shouldn't give up.
Exploration deserves two thumbs up.
Traveling near and far. Carrying around old battle scars.
Our strength will be renewed so we lift up our hands in prayer.
Angry about the circumstances
but knowing that life isn't always fair.
As we display a powerful faith
we should realize we're living our fate.
Stomping out problems which seem to never give up.
Just refuse to lie down.
No matter what.
Mountains and valleys are like buildings
and alleys that will hinder ones direction.
Move from our presence.
We still have a vision.
Yes we've made our decision.
To avoid all collisions.
To the occasion we have risen.
Freed from the prison.
So just refuse to give up until the day we die.
No matter what.

66

"Reminiscing"

The days are no longer long
because the thought of you quickens my heart.
Even though you're not physically present we're not apart.
I can recall the last events of our life together.
The sun was shinning above
so that our love has fair weather.
Can this be recorded as the best days of our lives?
The feeling is so remarkable
it is as if I've won the grand prize.
My heart is the chest that holds our friendship in safety.
I long for the day when you will again face me.
Think of it, there's going to be such a rejoicing.
In-separable we will be, never a thought of divorcing.
Always together in my thoughts.
For you've accepted me over looking my faults.
That reminds me, to be careful and fulfill your needs.
Forever reminiscing that you are with me.

67

"Embrace"

Touch me, such a warm embrace.
Hold me, until it shows on my face.
Kiss me, so that I can feel it within.
Love me, until it penetrates my skin.
This feeling flows so deep.
From the top of my head to the bottom of my feet.
Can we include love in this desire?
It has already been added, I can feel the fire.
The warmth of your embrace makes my body alive.
Yes, this is true I can not deny.
Wrap around me to keep me safe.
Engulf me within a special place.
Such a sweetheart it can only be grace.
It can never be enough so I'll hold on in case.
I am overwhelmed to say the least.
It is the embrace that gives me peace.
Yes there is faith that will never cease.
It can only be the embrace of someone, that is sweet.

68

"Ordinary"

Times may have changed but it is customary.
Nothing stays the same.
This thought is primary.
Change increases versatility.
Unlike the lack of can develop an air of hostility.
Being plain stands out just as bold.
It doesn't have to gleam just to be gold.
Thinking high of one's self is very necessary.
Who said it wasn't okay just being ordinary.
Ordinary comes from order meaning the proper state.
Now, up should rise self-esteem being basic we should elate.
Based upon a cover up, originality is not fake.
We are who we are so don't let that be a mistake.
Everyone can't be a peanut some of us have to be an almond.
If your regular then it's okay, being different is quite common.
Now that is that, a stated fact.
So if you're bald or hairy,
God loves all of us the same even though we are ordinary.

69

"Day Dream"

Sitting or standing one can fall into a conscious sleep.
Wondering about something or someone unique.
A thought or an idea holds our attention.
Never fading from our path frozen in suspension.
It is as if nothing else exists.
It can be a person, place, or thing as we reminisce.
Focus on an object visible or unseen.
Far from the night only in a daydream.
Pleasant can be the state of mind.
Peaceful is the thought suspended in time.
Uninterrupted by the events that surround our life.
Intoxicated by a thought that cuts like a knife.
Time goes on and there's no shame.
For the mind can freeze from frame to frame.
We float back to reality or is that how it seems?
Or is every thought just a day dream?

70

"Anymore"

I am not afraid anymore.
I know that I will be talked about.
I understand about me others will have their doubts.
I will not mistake myself for something I'm not.
I will be the best that I am, at what I plot.
I am not afraid anymore.
I will use my abilities to be me.
I mean that my limitations,
will obey when I'm down on my knee.
I will get up. I don't have to buff.
I realize that I have enemies that think killing me is ideal.
I know that I have power and it is real. I am sure.
I am not afraid anymore.
I take life serious.
I can be mysterious.
I know I'm not delirious.
I will give to the poor.
I will endure.
I am not afraid anymore.

71

"Pleasant Dreams"

As the day fades away our thoughts
are prepared for another day.
The star lights twinkle
and the moon gives off reflective light.
Children are tucked in,
while grown ups prepare for the night.
Destine for the sandman to close those weary eyes.
Lying to comfort the body the position is compromised.
Silent is home surrounded by peace.
Blessed is a person that receives a good nights sleep.
On through the night our minds will wonder.
Even in the mist of a storm unaware of the thunder.
So engulfed into happier themes
while you sleep I wish you pleasant dreams.

72

"Use to Be"

Impure and filthy, tattered and torn.
No more of that I've been reborn.
The renewal of m mind, body and soul.
What can stop my mission now that I'm on a roll.
Be rooted real deep so you can grow steadily.
Saved is what we are damned is what we use to be.
Prepare to stand on the truth for this there's no fee.
It is wise to accept your own responsibility.
Watch my tongue. "Naw, that aint me."
I'd better before I end up desperate ready to make a plea.
I like it right. It's better to stay away from wrong.
I thought the days were short and the nights were oh, so long.
Now I sang a new song.
No more back and forth like a ping pong.
I look at time differently and peace really suits me.
It is good to feel brand new
because old is what I use to be.

73

"Happy Being Me"

Oh, what a feeling it is to be free.
I was bound now I'm just happy being me.
Loneliness has no place in my life.
I've been granted the opportunity just to make it right.
Whatever it takes there's no fuss.
If my car broke down I would catch the bus.
No sweat, that's just how it's going to be.
Alive and well just happy being me.
Abandoned and broke,
lost without hope,
abusive with dope.
That's no joke but I had to cope.
So I remembered a quote.
"The truth will set you free."
I believe so that's why I'm happy being me.
I was lost but now I'm found.
My life is now safe and sound.
I was blind but now I can see.
I am happy being me.
Love is in me now I refuse to hate.
I've learned to have patience that means I will wait.

Peace I feel.
Salvation is real.
In prayer I will kneel.
That's the deal.
My smile is my plea for all to see.
I'm happy being me.

"Thankful"

There are so many things around us to be thankful about.
I'm so thankful I could just shout.
Shouts of joy echoing through my lungs.
Remembering our Savior on the cross as the hung.
There's appreciation for everyday things.
I am thankful to be alive just like
the birds all day when they sing.
I've learned not to expect but to wait
and see what life will bring.
It's made up of the same thankfulness
that a wife has when her husband buys her a ring.
I'm thankful for the flowers nor can I forget the bee's.
I'm thankful for this hour because I'm still able to breathe.
Many days I've noticed the clouds rolling through the sky.
If I have a task to complete then I'm thankful just to try.
I am thankful for all things that bring joy because I care.
For this I'll stay thankful and thankfulness I will share.

75

"Together"

Just think of it nothing can come between us.
I'll give you my confidence as well as my trust.
We'll stand against all things
that try to separate our relationship.
We are close as Siamese twins joined by the hip.
Wherever I go you are in my heart.
Our ties are so strong what can pry us apart?
When I call on you, you are there.
You are unlike some friend whom I can't compare.
I can't explain why our bond is so deep.
Could it be because we want to be together
everyday of the week.
If I had one dollar for every thought
that I have about you.
Then I would be a billionaire and that is true.
I have an idea, lets celebrate our life forever.
I'll be with you and you with me, meaning together.

76

"Circumstances"

Victimized or unintentional, direct or coincidental.
Are bad circumstances preventable?
That's a question answered sometimes with,
"I don't know?"
Though I do understand that without
certain events progress will not grow.
"What for?" "How come?" "Why me?"
"Why not you, can't you see?
Circumstances in my life have been personal
so that I can overcome any condition.
Oh, by the way did I mention that one must listen.
Just in case the same events slap someone in the
face. If this occurs, use wisdom to avoid disgrace.
So opposing the bad conditions mercy
and justice will serve as a petition.
It's a win, win situation when understanding is set in place.
So that means that every circumstance is guarded by Grace.
Don't leave things for luck or even good chances.
But let it be known that everyone
can overcome opposing circumstances.

77

"Counting Your Steps"

Before we are born all life
is predestined for a particular purpose.
I realized that there is guidance for
a man so no need to fuss.
You can go to and fro as long as you stay
within a boundary.
There are rules that apply for all to live
by just make sure that it is morally.
If you walk left when you are suppose to walk right.
You may end up in the wrong place
that is dark as the night.
There are pits and traps set in your life
so escaping to prayer helps.
Believe that your prayers will be answered
because someone is counting your steps.

78

"Love"

Many wonderful things result in love.
Just like the season of spring
that gives the earth an affectionate hug.
This is a gift that makes us grow fond of one another.
I will search to the ends of the earth,
for love I will discover.
It is understood that love is an action
which is something we all should do.
I understand what its' purpose
is because love is described in the truth.
Love is patient, love is kind, it always protects,
and it always trust.
Love always hopes and perseveres it
never fail and this is a must.
This gift of endearment is all that some people got.
This is what I give to you,
so out of love this is what it's not.
Love doesn't envy or even boast and it is not proud.
It is not rude, it is not self seeking meaning selfish,
self centered and loud.

Love has no temper and keeps no record of wrong.
It does not delight in evil but rejoices
in the truth all day long.
This now ends my description
which comes from above.
If we can handle the truth then we too can be in love.

79

"Persevere"

The marathon seems long and your hurting at the hip.
The waves seem like their going
to crash the boat but don't abandon ship.
Just intend to grow like the passing of another year.
Remember to never to give up continue to persevere.
We must go the full distance until the very end.
Be diligent and eager, we should always play to win.
There are two rules to success,
they are steadfast and perseverance.
If we can't see the path then blink until the way is clear.
The right way of doing things mean
that you are sure of what to do.
Our destiny is right before us, it is up to us to purse.
Our muscle do not become strong until we build them up.
"You can't teach an old dog new tricks,"
it easier to teach a pup.
Put some faith into your self and don't leave it to luck.
If you try over and over again perseverance will fill your cup.

80

"Versatility"

I can live a life full and effective.
I am always on the positive, I steer far from the negative.
If I had to switch over to another leaf.
I would do it in a heart beat.
If it need be, I will run or I will walk.
I can be silent or I can talk.
If it's cold outside then I would wear a coat.
There's no price on what I know but I will give a quote.
I don't just count the miles I can learn about kilometers.
I don't eat vegetables alone I am also a meat eater.
There are multiple ways of doing things.
This makes me available to make a change.
The more I lack the more I need recruits.
If it doesn't come to me then knowledge is my pursuit.
There is nothing in this world that can amount to my ability.
Who can put a price on a person with versatility?

81

"Enthused"

Captured by the idea that some things are delightful.
Engulfed in pleasures that is treasure to the insightful.
Being devoted in doing the best can bring on such a thrill.
Discerning in full knowledge is understanding ones' will.
One can be pleased with another
by showing them how they feel.
Always be ready to please, eager to keep it real.
We can be over taken when love is not mistaken.
Excited by the way we feel.
Giving our all, out of zeal.
Stay excited to please and eager to put at ease.
Which means to be committed.
Dedicated and always with it.
If it is something you delight in and the feeling is extreme.
Be devoted to make it right, it is real not a dream.
There is willingness, eagerness and dedication when enthused.
If fulfillment is what you seek then love can't be over ruled.

82

"Compare"

I have looked high and low but no one came compare to you.
Ever since I knew it would last my interest grew.
Love showed me what I should always do.
So now every day it is you that I pursue.
Next to you none is more beautiful.
You must be held in honor, now that's an eye full.
Equality means the same.
But compared to you, you are more than plain.
I've considered what is best for me.
The day I opened my eyes was the day I was able to see.
You've brought sunshine to my days and chased away the rain.
Spite all of the hardship loving you can heal the pain.
You are interesting, with you I am not board.
You are mine, love enter winds like a three strand cord.
I will defend your honor like a knight
yielding a double edged sword.
So to the death I prepare. Of course, I care.
Nothing else can compare to the love that we share?

83

"It's All on Me"

It took some time for me to figure this one out. I just
received the instructions on what life is really about.
Share and love, share and love these are two
good instructions that fit like hand in glove.
We have tough choices to make, would you agree?
I can't wait for some one else to do it, it's all on me.
Don't put off until tomorrow what one can
get done today. Take all necessary precau-
tions if obstacles are in the way.
Rejoice in the mornings and pray for a bet-
ter night. Since I've found out that it's all on me,
I know that my troubles will be in for a fight.
Do not be arrogant but show humil-
ity instead. If you're faced with embarrassment
then shame won't hover over your head.
We must love ourselves, again would you agree? I've
said it once and I'll say it again," It's all on me.

84

"How's it Going"

Excuse me friends.
I was just wondering. "How 's it Going?"
You don't have to answer, caring is all that I'm doing.
I had just notice that you're disturbed by something.
What can I do to help and don't tell me nothing.
Guess what? I'm about to share a little advice.
If you take heed and realize that faith works.
Believing the truth never hurts.
Don't expect because matters don't always go our way.
Before we make any critical decisions
I suggest that we pray.
Do we have faith enough to believe in the living God?
What about all of the unexplainable events
that are miracles, "Why is it odd ?"
I asked how it's going just in case you
needed to know if someone still cared.
Certainly someone does, in that area I'm well prepared.
My heart goes with you whatever you are doing.
If you take the advice that I gave,
then good is how it's going.

85

"Bless the Babies"

Bless them so that they won't suffer loss.
Yes, care for them at all cost.
I am a man so that means that I will protect the young.
I would guide all the children of the world
if other men wouldn't take care of their young.
I 'm for real, just ask my kids
they'll tell you that their father's number one.
There's no question that I'm professing
to be the man that gets it done.
Bless the babies and adore them like daisies.
Give them shelter, some food, sunshine and lots of hugs.
Show them that we care with actions of love.
Bless the babies give them guidance in their youth.
Plant seeds of knowledge, wisdom and truth.
Teach them discernment so that they will understand that
caring for the little ones is a privilege and a command.
Say yes, not maybe.
"All men and women should, bless the babies."

 ALAN ALSTON SR.

86

"Prolific"

Is a word that means fruitful.
It's a description of how we should live.
"Now that's beautiful."
People should not be idle, stagnant or living dead.
We are supose to live in fullness
believing that Christ is the head.
I'm not trying to convert anyone but the truth will convict.
There's only one name that will either bring joy
to the heart or it'll make a non-believer sick.
Just remember that for the rest of our lives
we are to live like trees that bear fruit.
The world is the orchard and judgment is in pursuit.
If the trees are prolific meaning producers
of fruit then this is good.
Opposite of that, one day there will come
the ax that cuts down useless tree for wood.
So if you're fruitful then keep producing higher and higher.
But to those that have termites in their wood,
I suggest that you watch for the ax
because after that, comes the fire.

87

"Continuation"

The definition means to flood a nation
with an influential occupation.
Prolongation is continual so that
I will always have the things I need for survival.
Now I am able.
I'm constantly seeking after ways
to maintain a lavish life style.
Providing that my efforts are not vain
I invest in integrity and profile.
It doesn't last just for a while.
That means I will always hustle, somehow.
Large capital comes with the work that
I put into continuation of my destiny.
Now through infinity notes that forever, is what works for me.
My optimistic ability to get revenue flows like clock work,
following in order having a domino effect.
From one extreme to the next.
Continually protected by a willingness
to keep on and succeed.
Now my existence is a continuation
of my destiny so I've planted my seed.
I reap what I sow, so that my gain is nice.
The duration of my existence is life.

88

"The Only Way"

I can't hold back my tongue because I have something to say.
No matter how much we want to do things our way.
Our decisions will be blessed only if we believe and pray.
This means to have faith in the truth
which is the only way.
We have been provided with obstacles and lies that deceive.
The only way to the truth is to believe.
It has been taught that the way is narrow.
But even the poorest person is looked
after and feed like the sparrow.
We categorize people in one or two ways,
there is either or there is or.
You either don't know or you are sure.
The only way is to endure.
So out of the truth comes love that is pure.
Walk in a way that is approved by righteousness.
If it is not then it could lead to lifelessness.
We have the option to choose
and one of them can exercise our say.
But there are consequences to our actions
when sin comes into play.
Just always be on guard and make this one a better day.
It is always worth the effort when love is the only way.

89

"Faithful"

I am this only when I put all,
I mean all of my trust into something
or someone I believe in.
If I have faith now will I have it then?
Of course I will,
only the faithful meaning full of faith, is loyal.
Even a servant puts its' confidence into the
hands of the master, treating him royal.
Faith is trust but without trust how can a situation end up just.
Right? Just a little insight.
The only thing that penetrates darkness is the light.
So that the day is faithful to change the night.
There's a sincere direction that a person must choose.
So stand firm if your choice is to remain
faithful otherwise you will lose.
There's either don'ts or do's and even rejoicing or the blues.
Whatever you decide being faithful is the glue.
It holds together a relationship
that is on the brink.
Being faithful is to be attached to a
promise like a strong link.

Nothing can break apart the bond
of the faithful except for disbelief.
The confidence is all in faith,
so where the faithful are there's a guarantee of relief.

90

"Achieve"

Set your mind on the goal then make every effort to reach it.
Walk the ways of the light because success is no dark secret.
You can do it, just get use to it,
a positive attitude is what you need.
Do not be discouraged, use your courage, you can achieve.
Go right ahead and believe, just as you will to breath.
Now is your turn to retrieve, what you came to achieve.
It is yours, so claim your victory because failure will deceive.
You have the ability just like anyone, you can achieve.
You are good just believe that there's no need to grieve.
Can you perceive, that you can be at ease?
The mind can deceive. Bringing your efforts to its' knees.
The effort to obtain is not in vain.
The accomplishments are the same
when one chooses to believe.
What can stop the plans of a man
that is destine to achieve?

 ALAN ALSTON SR.

91

"Conqueror"

Circumstances, situations and troubles
do not dictate the outcome of my life.
You are more than a conqueror,
for we triumph over strife.
Victorious champions that walk a path that is right.
Able to be at peace, care free if approached by a fight.
Live as if the battle has already been won.
Our strength comes from above
so that Gods' will be done.
There's spiritual warfare between the body and the soul.
Credited righteousness and salvation should be the goal.
Prove yourself loyal only to the truth.
Let no one still your joy or the innocence of the youth.
Doubt not but contend with faith.
Study to show your self approved,
then your destined to be great.
Be patient it is said that,
"A wise person can endure the wait."
You are more than a conqueror
because victory seals your fate.

92

"Love me"

Love me for who I am not for what I'm <u>WORTH.</u>
Love me like I am the only one you
care for upon this <u>EARTH.</u>
Love me when I am <u>RIGHT.</u>
Love me when I am <u>WRONG.</u>
Love me when you sang that special love <u>SONG.</u>
Love me like your heart is where I <u>Belong.</u>
Love me when I need a <u>HUG.</u>
Love me with unconditional <u>LOVE.</u>
Love me with excitement and <u>BLISS.</u>
Love me with your passionate <u>KISS.</u>
Love me if you get the <u>URGE.</u>
Love me when I get on your <u>NERVE.</u>
Love me in your <u>MIND.</u>
Love me all of the <u>TIME.</u>
Love me in your <u>HEART.</u>
Love me when we are <u>APART.</u>
Love me until the <u>END.</u>
Love me and we will <u>WIN.</u>
Understand that this is the way that it must <u>Be.</u>
Forever through whatever with someone that loves <u>ME.</u>

93

"Thinking for Myself"

Sometime has passed and no more crying for help.
I'm all grown up now so I'm thinking for myself.
I don't have to fear, so I don't.
I can see things real clear, shut my eyes, I won't.
Subjected to persecution for who I am, brings discuss.
My strength comes from up above, so I trust.
I am thankful for the time that
I am here in the life that I dwell.
I got my mind right now,
I'm thinking for myself.
Exposed to crime, drugs and sex I've made some habits.
All innocence is preyed upon like
the predator hunts the rabbits.
Out of the natural order caged behind bars and locked doors.
It's not likely for the rich but it's designed for the poor.
I've made my way, day by day, pray I say.
It is the only way to escape moral decay.
The wise one will listen, this means pay attention.
Taking heed is in order, it will bring help. Time is
getting shorter, so I started thinking for myself.

"Stable"

Unmoved, unshaken is my foundation.
So there's no need for explanation.
Preoccupation about my affiliation, sadly mistaken.
Negative offense but none taken.
My roots are deep so that makes it difficult
to uproot any may planted with Gods' own hands.
I grow so that my fruit is tasted all over the land.
Understand that my faith has made me able.
The one that created me has marked my heart with a label.
Ever since I was detached at the navel.
The truth has been told, far from a fable.
My strength is renewed,
rejuvenated like being hooked to a cable.
He has dressed me with wisdom
and invited me to sit at his table.
These are the last days so the shepherd
gathers his flock into his stable.

95

"Sincerity"

Direct all of your attention to what is correct.
Recollect that one must earn some respect.
This is the way to acquire a position that is select.
Honest intention will not bring regret.
A genuine heart does insure the soul of the lost.
After all the price is sweet, a change is all that is cost.
Thinking pure thoughts one will be blessed beyond measure.
A sincere heart is such a great treasure.
Submitting only to true love one will receive the pleasure.
Dishonest motives only lead to death.
Renew the mind before the very last breath.
Stay focused on things that are real.
Because the deceiver will tempt us
with things that have appeal.
In this state of honesty being true makes life clear.
Of course there will be let downs but nothing to fear.
Mistakes will be made,
so you can take that to the bank.
There's a freedom from hypocrisy it's called sincerity,
"Now that's frank."

96

"Your Touch"

It is unexplainable the way that I feel.
When I have felt your touch, I knew that all of this is real.
It's so firm but oh so gentle.
You are mine far from some trophy on the mantle.
I appealed to you and you granted me a sample.
You move my heart and that's just one example.
There's no sweeter desire that the feel of your touch.
You've caused me to believe in love
and that's worth oh so much.
Priceless is the gift that you gave.
I know of nothing else that can compare.
It took some time for me to see but now I am aware.
I wasn't able to see all of these things because I wasn't wise.
I understand now because with you there are tries.
It is always hello and no more good-byes.
So I thank you for your touch,
it is your love that opens my eyes.

97

"Able"

Why? Why are you not? Who said that you wasn't? Surely?
I am almost definite that it's a lie.
Believe that you can then step out on faith and do try.
Really, you are. I know that you can.
Believe that it's all part of a divine plan.
You are capable to do all things whether small or great.
Can you relate?
There should be no giving up.
For what? Just because you got awe struck.
Then you thought that it was bad luck.
Poor thing, that's just passing the buck.
You will be? You'll see. It's not by power or by might.
That's a physical fight. Alright?
It is by the grace of the spirit.
Did you hear it? So once again,
"Child of the Most High," will be your label.
Only because through Him all things are able.

98

"Kisses of Gold"

I took out this time to express
the way that I feel about your sweet kisses.
There so precious that I've put them
at the top of my wishes.
The value of your love has no equal.
It takes my breath away so I will confess to all people.
What could be the price to pay for kisses of gold?
Loving expressions like this could never be sold.
When I look into your eyes I just want to embrace your lips.
If there is punishment for the love
I have then I would endure being beat by whips.
So I will contend to win and stand like a lion so bold.
Because in the end I will again enjoy your kisses of gold.
Feelings like this will never cease.
When we come together I am blessed to say the least.
It's written in your eyes with that loving stare.
You know exactly what I mean
so nothing else can compare.
I agree to take our time but my feelings I can not hold.
Come to me then you'll see that
I to have, "Kisses of Gold."

99

"Reasons"

In life there are destinations.
So when we give our reasons
we should have explanations.
The reason I love is because I can not hate.
If I want it now then sometimes I have to wait.
The reasons we have to wait is to teach us patience,
understanding and endurance.
If we succeed on our course
then we've experienced perseverance.
It is always proper to be polite.
The reason being is because it's right.
The reason we pray is because of belief.
The reason some have followers
is because a staff has a chief.
Go forward only to never turn back.
Because if you turn around
the you might not stay on track.
Do not associate with others
not of the same frame of mind.
The reason being is if they fall
into trouble then you might be in the same bind.

So seek wisdom and discernment
during all four seasons.
Only then will you know
that prosperity and success will be the reasons.

100

"Waiting on You"

In this life we are taught that there will be
tough times that will come to cause us grief.
This doesn't bother me because it is from you
that I'm granted peace.
So if it doesn't come right away
I will be waiting on you for relief.
"Who are you?" this is a question that I have to address.
You are the creator of all things, my Lord whom I profess.
I look to the sky and know that my help comes real soon.
Who better to wait on than the one who created
the sun and the moon.
You are the, "King of Kings,"
the "Lords or Lords," and the, "Bright and Morning Star."
Your name is Jesus, that's who you are.
When I did seek you
I was on my own and didn't know what to do.
Trouble was at my door step so I called on you.
You taught me faith to believe that I'm okay.
For you are the way.
This I've learned and I can discern
that you hold things together tight live glue.

Thank you for the ideas,
direction and all those simple little clues.
All men can be saved whether Gentile or Jew.
You are my Savior so I'm waiting on no one, but you.

101

"Safe"

There are rules to abide by and every participant has a place.
If you follow them correctly there'll be safe passage by grace.
Be patient because everyone receives there turn.
Some will strike out but for others
there will be lessons that they'll learn.
Step up and plant your feet solid to the ground.
Keep your eyes on deception
because the enemy is on the mound.
You may have to duck so do it with precision.
Remember what you have practiced
so that you can make the right decision.
Then you can move to the first position
but you have to freeze.
Wait for some help then the next step you will be pleased.
Do not boast for the most part and begin to tease.
There are two more positions
and the third one will put you at ease.
Reflect back to the rules.
They are valuable tools.
Don't look to the sides.
Keep your eyes on the prize.

Watch for distractions the next move depends on action.
Remain in a zone.
Run like the wind and when you hear
safe you've made it home.

102

"After the Rain"

There's much to gain.
So, use your brain.
All pleasure no pain.
Just the opposite of when Abel was killed by Cain.
That incident was profane.
Jealousy made him insane.
In so many words my friend I'll make it plain.
There's not always sunshine after the rain.
Do not hold on to your problems
allow them to flow down the drain.
Get rid of that old baggage break loose from that chain.
Move in the right direction that means go with the grain.
There are two pathways to follow
the alternative or the main.
If you chose the right one then your days
will be lifted high like a crane.
Making your life blessed with sunshine after the rain.
Optimism should be daily and negativity you must refrain.
Everyone has a purpose our lives are not in vain.
The Judge has taken his seat so everyone will be arraigned.

There will be ones that are lost and ones that are ordained.
This I believe for sure by faith, and my belief is sane.
I remember learning a Holy promise
that there will be a rainbow after the rain.

103

"Proclaim"

There is much to gain.
So use your brain.
All pleasure no pain.
Just the opposite of when Able was killed by Cain.
That incident was profane.
Jealousy made him insane.
So to you my friend I'll make it plain.
There isn't always sunshine after the rain.
Do not hold on to your problems
allow them to flow down the drain.
Get rid of that old baggage break loose from that chain.
Move in the right direction that means go with the grain.
There's two pathways to follow the alternative or the main.
If you choose the right one then your days
will be lifted high like a crane.
Making your life blessed with sunshine, after the rain.
Optimism should be daily and negativity you must refrain.
Everyone has a purpose our lives are not in vain.
The Judge has taken his seat so everyone will be arraigned.

The ones that are lost and the one's that are ordained.
This I know for sure, my faith is very sane.
Remember that Holy promise
when there's a rainbow, after the rain.

104

"Precious"

All through life I searched just to have someone
as precious as you.
If you asked me to be yours, undoubtedly I will say I do.
Wherever you may be you may be
I'll look to keep my eyes fixed like glue.
I suppose it's because I know your love will be true.
What could another do for me when you are worth so much.
The way you look at me feels as good as your touch.
Mend my heart with your love like it's a tool.
You make me feel at ease that's
why you are as precious as a jewel.
All of the past relationships we have had perished.
Just like you, this relationship will be cherished.
These words that I write come from the depths of my heart.
So I'll pray to the Lord if it's
His will we will never be apart.
I understand that we must take it easy
in our life style walking the straight and narrow.
But as soon as I get the opportunity
I have to thank cupid for shooting us with his arrow.

I will not stop until my prayers
have been answered from up above.
I know for sure now that I've found someone
as precious as you to always love.

105

"Each Day Is A New Day"

For the most part we all reflect back
upon the days that we can't have anymore.
Reminiscing about yesterday and the days before.
Most of us are not aware of what's going to be in store.
So we shut ourselves out unable to enjoy
a new day or an opened door.
Smile because yesterday you wore that old frown.
Live a life of love so in Gods' blessing you will drown.
Completely engulfed in peace
not even death can get you down.
Believe that each day is a new day
and tomorrow you might receive your crown.
People are not truly happy until we can find peace.
Pretending that everything is alright
when actually there's only grief.
Some days are orchestrated and not a wish of luck
like a clover leaf.
Each day is a new day so that means that there is relief.
The door will be opened when you knock
and you will find when you seek.
This gives a promise to strengthen those that are weak.
So collect yourself, "Each day is a new day,"
365 days a year, seven days a week.

106

"Crusin"

Asphalt far and wide so is the wisdom
of the one who created the tide.
Infinity meaning forever is the journey
form death to rebirth.
It's on ongoing experience,
cruising along with the King over all of the earth.
We've been taken into custody
that declares that our ransom has been paid.
Insured through eternity now
I can accept the way that I'm made.
Which is an easy going.
Knowledge knowing, forever showing that I'm a provider.
Crusin' through life so that makes me a rider.
All day and all night requests.
"For goodness sakes," my prayers are blessed.
The energy around me is positive just like a proton.
Steering from the negatives that are morons.
Main streets, back streets through valley and alleys.
Whether walking or riding or in Balley's or on Ralley's.
Living a peaceful life because I'm always at ease.
Cruisin' right on by cool like an artic breeze.

107

"For Us"

In this world that we live in there
are a lot of gifts that are taken for granted.
Look at our everyday scenery,
check out the greenery, that's been planted.
For us there is breath so we inhale.
If it wasn't for this gift then every human would turn pale.
There's a lot more to think about
like if there's injustice then will mercy prevail.
Or if we ask for forgiveness does it exempt us from hell.
Just have faith then all is well.
Consider what's been said because
I hit the head of nail.
For us, we have the reasons.
Nature knows the seasons.
For us there is we and for we that's the key.
United, don't you agree?
Take this literally word for word, life is copious.
Abundant are the gifts that are just for us.
So note this and write it upon your heart.
Love is for us all and love is where we start.
That's why there should never be a fuss.
Because, for us, "In God we trust."

108

"Highly Advisable"

Education is a recommended recommendation.
Without the proper knowledge
how could there be edification.
Strength goes to the muscles when the body works out.
Just as wisdom goes to the brain when
knowledge is roaming about.
Recapture the essence of life. Obedience
is better than sacrifice.
To consider what is right there must be an under-
standing of what is wrong. When we are
weak it is said that we are strong.
If faith is tested then it is strength that we
seek. Which makes strength the goal so
strong we are while we are weak.
Morality is regarded to right and wrong acts.
Withholding the truth brings about unethical fact.
Wisdom has brought enlightenment
so that virtue can answer the question, How?
With purity of the body, mind, language and style.
Now the truth has filled your thoughts
making it all undeniable.
Renewal of any kind is highly advisable.

109

"Who Ever Knew"

It certainly never crossed my mind.
That day I approached you I knew you where my kind.
It was plain what I saw when I looked in your face.
There was a spot that was free, so you've made it my place.
So now I rejoice because real love I've never had.
Just look at my face there is evidence that I'm glad.
People have seem to talk because love can come in two.
Yes it feels so right but who ever knew?
Life works so we could meet one another.
Your the type of person that
I would love to meet my mother.
You are dear, this I feel from inside my heart.
Yes it's clear it was real from the start.
Thanks to fate I no longer have to wait.
I now have a mate and that makes it great.
You please me, which makes it easy to say, I do.
I am yours and you are mine but who ever knew?

110

"Emotion"

Sometimes we all are disturbed
or agitated by someone or something.
When emotions flare up excitement is what it'll bring.
The mind will play on one's emotion.
Triggering anxiety as if it were a deadly potion.
Anxious to resolve a feeling for relief.
Irreversible events can bring about much grief.
The mind will be filled with great concern.
Life isn't about our feelings so this truth I had to learn.
Emotions can make us cry if we think of moving thoughts.
It will also make us lie if we cover up from getting caught.
Life can flow smooth like an aloe lotion.
If we keep in tuned to reality
and not give way to emotion.
Emotion describes agitation.
This is not organization.
The concept I bring is an idea or a notion.
So that there's remembrance not to be lead by your emotion.

111

"On My Mind"

Listen my love, there is not too many minutes in a day
that I don't think about us.
Truthfully and to me that's a plus.
Ticking like clock work is the time that
I put into our relationship.
I'll bend over backwards and do a back flip.
I can't read your mind or feel your heart.
So if love is true then we will never be apart.
Someone as real as you is so hard to find.
That's why you're always on my mind.
Excuse me, but I will tell the truth and that's no lie.
I won't get upset with you and don't explain why.
If you don't see my point then
I will have faith that you'll try.
It is obvious that you're willing but this is my reply.
If you can believe then let's see eye to eye.
I won't need another to care for me if
I ask you and you won't deny.
The things in the past I have left behind.
So that our love can spiritually bind.
Be with me forever and make our love one of a kind.
You're the only one I want, the only one on my mind.

112

"Take Your Time"

Slow down there's no need to rush into it.
Be patient when you pursue it.
Walk so that you can get a full view.
It's not smart to swallow whole bites,
first you have to chew.
Can you feed a new born baby table
food or do we give them milk?
So don't speed up just let it flow smooth like silk.
There can't be fulfillment at the drop of a dime.
Pleasant gifts will come if you take your time.
If you want it quick situations could lead to crime.
Freedom is a virtue just take your time.
Is there a love search or does it find us off guard.
A diamond at first is coal and only time can make it hard.
Trust is kind like lust is blind,
both of them need patience and both of them rhyme.
You can do it your way please take your time.
Tell yourself, who can stop a young champion
when they're in their prime?
Longevity made them successful and success comes,
when you take your time.

113

"Wisdom"

Learning can be reward and the neglect of it is
foolishness to someone that has prudence.
This gives a wise person the discretion
that knowledge has essence.
To imply this concept of truth
there must be a distinction of the facts.
Wisdom is gained by knowledge studied
by performance or by acts.
Being candid or outspoken
of a particular privilege is freedom.
So that the liberty of sound judgment
can manifest wisdom.
There is validity if the mind will succumb.
Then the truth can set us free and through
wisdom the body can overcome.
Even a fool can be shrewd but only to deceive.
Only a sagacious believer will be quick to perceive.
Sagacity is quickness of discernment
making us crafty in our thoughts.
Granting us high intelligence to recognize our faults.
The facts have been presented so to the
truth the wise person, will come.
Granted all that is sought to obtain, more wisdom.

"Pray for Me"

I am in duress so I long for relief.
Heavy is my heart all I carry around is grief.
The day is long it seems as if time did freeze.
What would make my heart feel at ease?
Could I ask a favor of you please?
Would you say a prayer for me?
You influence me with such a warm attitude.
Now I am thankful with much gratitude.
How wonderful it is to have you on my side.
I asked for a favor which wasn't denied.
You are there for me whether far or wide.
Love like this you can not hide.
You and I, friend we'll always be.
"No more wondering, why?" because you will pray for me.
Thanks to your prayers I've been set free?
It's because of faithfulness that I'm able to see.
I understand now that prayer is the key.
It will solve any problem from A to Z.
If you see me stumble then remember my plea.
I will stand tall if you agree, to pray for me.

115

"Innocence"

Be a person with a simple heart
so that the things that are wrongful keep you innocent.
Approach evil like a child is what that statement meant.
Wickedness is nonsense.
Hold on to the rest of your innocence.
If you trifle in dirt then one is said to be "dirty."
Just because we want to remain clean
doesn't make someone, "nerdy."
Does moral decay make any sense?
A noxious attitude does make a difference.
Freedom from crime or guilt will bring confidence.
this freedom describes innocence.
A innocent person displays prudence.
A new attitude toward life making love the essence.
It will bring any person some relief if there is acceptance.
Now gather what's being taught
so that in liberty you can choose what is free.
Being a slave to guilt must no longer be.
We are refined in life so that we can walk in elegance.
Keeping far from sin is to live in innocence.

116

"Victory"

Give a victory shout and have confidence
that you've already won.
Keep your head held high so that other's
will know that it's been done.
Rejoice because we're on the winning team.
Realizing great potential it is exactly how it might seem.
Gaining the prize is the description of this theme.
We are more than conquerors so that victorious
conquest isn't a dream.
March on for the sake of receiving what's due.
It depends on our attitude so that it is left up to you.
Each individual must stand their own ground.
So that when you stand firm perseverance shall be found.
A race is ran but only the winner receives the prize.
Keep your focus a head of you like there are no more tries.
Go on as if there are no more chances
so that this will make you wise.
A champion knows that the finish is near
even if they can't see it with their own eyes.
The ending will be marked so that
the faithful will go down in history.
Only those that believe in a better day
will receiver true victory.

117

"Milk and Honey"

These nouns describes a fruitful land.
For those that inhabit it the harvest must be grand.
Silk and money are like milk and honey.
The first two are smooth and the last are sweet.
They all will benefit the body as well as grant us a treat.
Milk nourishes the body while honey gives us joy.
Stay far away from greed I mean other wise be coy.
In life there are hidden treasures.
So we seek them out to fulfill our pleasures.
Thanks to this divine gift we have hope
that our day will be sunny.
Given to us because of Grace we are
blessed with milk and honey.

118

"Strong Foundations"

How can any structure stand
without having first been made.
Through any situation a strong foundation has to be laid.
We have buildings constructed to view
as the eyes would see a church.
The church is an elevated position placed
in our hearts for the truth to perch.
Storing up a little at a time in a savings account
will harvest secured placement.
Strong foundations give us security in a storm
so we go to the lower level of a building or a basement.
People exist through the base that's been laid
which are our parents.
They guide their young away from death
which is visually apparent.
Morals, a job, and a basic education
are the basis of a strong foundation.
Every individual needs these types of motivation.
Righteousness is a career.
Did you hear?
All of our lives we must build up.

Not until we wake up.
For our sakes we receive breaks of mercy from divine acts.
Divine intervention is all that I've known as fact.
Submit to the righteousness that's in you
granted un- limited range.
Live a lifestyle built on strong foundations of change.
You know it's there, you can feel it like the wind.
Keep building up what is right until the very end.

119

"Day by Day"

For all that it is worth read the words
on this page or listen to what I say.
Our lives are renewed, day by day.
Each day we awake we should be thankful
to feel the warmth of life, in every way.
Our lives produce a shine, day by day.
Do not settle fo' less.
If you want the best.
Command the rest to get out of the way.
Work to be stronger, day by day.
Use the same amount of effort that we put into a days pay.
So that we receive blessing, day by day.
In the same way we must pray.
Requesting that we don't gain the world
but that our needs are met, day by day.
Be that as it may.
Put your faith into perseverance, day by day.
We can fly and sing all day long just like the blue jay.
Birds are an example, they show us freedom
and joy so we must claim peace, day by day.

Be on guard for whatever comes into play.
Humans are prey for the spirit world, day by day.
Evil spirits will haunt us if we don't obey.
Every life has a purpose so you must find yours,
search day by day.
The Potter made the water jug out of a lump of clay.
We have been made to be who we are going to be,
which is our privileged, day by day.

120

"I Beseech Thee"

Stay in school, I beseech thee.
Don't company with a fool, I beseech thee.
Do your very best.
Never ever settle to take only the rest, I beseech thee.
Get more not less.
Eliminate the stress, I beseech thee.
Seek wisdom and truth.
Obtain knowledge to share with the youth, I beseech thee.
Train up our kids in the proper manner.
Display your life like a flag or a banner, I beseech thee.
Be an example for others to see.
I will pray for you and you bray for me, I beseech thee.
Do me a favor? Love your neighbor, I beseech thee.
Stand for all that is right.
Gain insight, I beseech thee.
Train for endurance.
Keep going through for perseverance, I beseech thee.
Don't rush, just take your time.
Be sweet and not lime, I beseech thee.
Stay at peace, meaning keep far from strife.

Renew the mind and claim back your life,
I beseech thee.
For these things I beg,
to your heart they may reach.
Through love I teach,
to the listener I beseech.

"Faith Not Hope"

Of the two, one will give confidence
and the other one only gives desires with an expectation.
Faith exceeds hope but they have a relation.
Faith is being sure of what we hope for.
Hope is expecting for what's in store.
It is wise to believe in the good than to just want the good.
It can be done, of course it could.
It will not or will it.
Be confident much more, why settle for a little bit?
Don't just want happiness, believe in joy.
A man is confident that he's a man
when he has matured from a boy.
We can believe that we will see another day.
So, can we hope that we'll make it all the way?
Of course one can hope. It is better to have faith
and not hope so we can cope.
We are given security when knowing for sure.
We hope for the best when there isn't a cure.
In times of need we should live by faith, not by sight.
In hope we have to see if everything will be alright.
By faith a bill will get paid, in hope there may remain a debt.
Faith means we can claim it now, hope implies not yet.

122

"Self"

Hello, how are you doing today?
Well, however you feel,
I suggest that you take care of yourself.
You are the only one that understands you.
Self, take good care of you.
I myself need you to look deep inside
so that you can find yourself.
Do for yourself the justice that you deserve.
Allow you full potential to display how you should serve.
Have you heard?
Self is only for letters but it's a mighty big word.
I just want you to soar high like a bird.
Of course, you can stop keeping up with the Jones;
it doesn't make you a nerd.
You're different that's why I love you.
Your spirit comes from up above.
One day you will leave this earth.
Your destiny has been recorded since the day of your birth.
No more selfish moves it only brings hurt.
Do yourself a favor and remember what you're worth.

There's no amount of money that can buy a person joy.
Don't play; life's no toy.
Self, you are growing; you're no longer a kid.
Adult is your thinking; wise is your counsel.
Outside of you there's love.
Inside you, you'll find peace.
Oh, how I love what you have to offer, such great wealth.
With you there's enough for everyone
to love because you will give yourself.

123

"Draw From Within"

Obedience draws a financial dividend.
Muster up all power and draw from within.
Health is having a sound state of body and mind, stable.
Wealth means riches, affluence, abundance or able.
To have the proper strength one exercises to grow strong.
This development requires discipline to help us get along.
Through our days we can produce again and again.
Observing what's right keep us far away from sin.
The right choices are destine to help us win.
If we submit to the spirit then draw from within.
We all are born in this world with the same opportunity.
Alone we are poor but together we are rich in unity.
We perform our duties to receive our lot.
Which is our portion in life and this is all that we've got.
All are valuable because we've been bought for a price.
It's a gift from on high, " Now isn't that nice?"
There is truth in us all which is a dividend.
The spirit is the provider of your share
of life if we draw from within.

124

"Warriors Prepare"

Everyone has heard of peace and war.
I say to you prepare for what's in store.
Put on the full armor of God so that you can stand
against the devils' schemes.
Warriors are subjected to all conditions
of evil intent under great extremes.
There are warriors of truth and warriors of a lie.
The ones' that fight on the side of truth never die.
Stand firm with the belt of truth buckled around your waist.
Be forever ready in haste.
With the breast plate of righteousness in place,
soldiers will be carried by grace.
Have your feet fitted with readiness
that comes from the gospel of peace.
Having zeal that never cease.
Be aware, all warriors prepare.
Also take with you the shield of faith so you can
extinguish all of the flaming arrows from the evil one.
Peace will not come until Gods' will be done.
Cover your head with the helmet of salvation.
There is redemption for ever nation.

And last of all take the sword of he spirit
which is the word of God so you can strike.
Warriors prepare so that you will know
what victory is like.

125

"Overlook"

Suppose that we have gotten ourselves in a bind.
We will run for a little comfort,
wanting relief is on our mind.
Consider any problems that may get into
your neighbors path.
No one should add more trouble,
when forgiveness is to be the math.
Remember that one day you might want the same relief.
Give all of the time but don't take like a thief.
Imagine if someone always stole your joy.
It would hurt like as if we were children
and what was taken was a favorite toy.
So watch what we say to other and the things we do.
Because what goes around comes around
and it will come back to you.
Have you ever wondered how life would
be if you won something good not once but twice.
That's the same feeling we should have about others,
some one has to be nice.
Explore the possibilities like learning a fun game.
If we expect forgiveness then we should do the same.

 ALAN ALSTON SR.

Focus, I mean set your mind on a better view.
If we can't forgive someone then
why should someone forgive us too.
See my point, it's like catching a fish on a hook.
If people are sorry or not shouldn't we still overlook?

126

"Dependant"

A pet depends on its' master just as aid
is needed after a disaster.
It is not proper to be self reliant.
We should be dependant on the Lord,
if not then it's defiant.
"Ask and you shall receive."
If you trust in what has been stated then you believe.
It is wise to live by faith and not by sight.
Belief is not a struggle or a fight.
"Seek and you shall find."
So if you are looking for help then
you're exercising an open mind.
Having faith in what you do not see is far from being blind.
If one is dependant then a rescuer
must save them from a bind.
Being dependant is a token.
It points out that a bond can not be broken.
So rely on the truth when it has been spoken.
"Knock and the door shall be open."
If one has to knock then doesn't it mean
that he door could be locked.

 Alan Alston Sr.

This states that our admittance has been blocked.
So the door has to be unlocked
by some one on the other side.
Making all dependant on deliverance
which can not be denied.

127

"Measure the Depth"

Can it be measured by human standards with precision?
Isn't wisdom a conscious decision.
To measure the oceans depth science use sound and radar.
The depth of outer space no one knows how far.
Imagination can take us to a much broader space.
So we can't measure that depth because reality is the case.
What may be real for me may not be real for some.
I've choose an optimistic view knowing
truth is where reality comes from.
Give a thought or account to a certain incident.
How, by going over the possible reasons
we may find out what it could have meant.
We have life with endless possibilities facing us everyday.
So we must measure our limitations
and strengths for a more peaceful way.
This approach gives life a meaning to live.
It's better not to receive but to give.
"Measure the depth," to the extreme
because life is what it seems.
Nothing easy comes for free,
that's why wisdom will measure things that we see.

128

"From A Father"

Hello my child, how are you doing today?
I took out this time because I have something to say.
You may not see me as often as I would like too.
So I want you to know that I am there for you.
You are with me forever in my heart everywhere I go.
You are my seed so I water you so that you will grow.
I have much to offer you but nothing is greater than love.
I found out the meaning of fatherhood
when you were given to me from up above.
I'll pray for your safety so that life won't get you down.
I've learned how to swim so that
I can teach you not to drown.
Listen to my instructions so that you will do what is right.
Everyone has some trouble but you must use your might.
Do your best to follow what is good too.
Not because I've said so but it's what we are going to do.
I know that there is goodness inside
of you that is more powerful than a flood.
The reason I can be sure of this is
because we share the same blood.
I love you that's why I bother,
blessings from your father.

129

"Smile"

Just do it because it's worth the while.
If you could make it a distance then it would be a mile.
If it could be a time of day then it would be called morning.
Life begins again so that it will end loud snoring.
So smile because life without one in so boring.
Sunshine will take its' place
stopping the rain from pouring.
Life is like nine hundred and
ninety nine hundred grand plus one more.
I say smile so that you will allow your
neighbor to know what a smile is for.
It is to give others joy and make our bodies health.
Be a person that smiles a lot because that person's wealth.
Your smile can not be taken away
if you haven't decided that it could leave.
A smile most of the time isn't hard for us to achieve.
Even if you have not teeth and
all you can do is show gums.
Just smile until you feel it in you heart
because a smile can relieve like tums.

130

"Receive Me"

The approach for acceptance starts with humble intent.
Humility in a situation can bring peace to an incident.
If I call for help and I'm in need.
Will there be an answer, "Let me know," is what I pled.
When there is love then committed is what it will be.
That's my whole point wouldn't you agree?
Isolated, separated and solitude how can one feel at ease?
Only from the comfort of peace. "Can I have it please?"
Accept me for who I am because I too have faults.
Reassure me of all my doubts
and take away the bad thoughts.
I don't mean to beg, I just have to see.
If you'll accept my proposal when I'm down on my knee.
What I have to offer is dedication to love without a fee.
Life is give or take, but to give is the key.
I will give my time, my all and do my best.
If we are one then I know you will do the rest.
As I am, I pray that you'll receive me.
It will make me very happy if you'll believe me.

131

"Star Chaser"

Star chaser, star chaser your dream has taken flight.
Go after it as quickly as you can
before the end of the night.
Dream of new ideas and always think of a happy thought.
Day light approaches bringing night dreams to a halt.
High flying adventures and winning the grand prize.
These things do come true, right before our eyes.
The pursuit of happiness is in everyone's dream.
Always be a team player while moving ahead, full steam.
Keep your mind in motion kike a shooting star.
Let nothing get in your way the you will go far.
Reach for the stars, chase them whom ever you are.
One day you might catch one and even keep it in a jar.
Go out and catch yourself a star
but be sure to use positive insight.
No matter how dark it may get
that star will shine so bright.
Then you can find your direction because
you have followed the light.
A star chaser will achieve if their light
can penetrate the night.

132

"A Special Place"

When it comes to peace it is like playing hide and seek.
It can't be found on the tree tops or a mountain peek.
In any case it is hope for the meek.
Being kind is grace, it is not weak.
Base all views upon a foundation of strength.
Chase away the blues by going the full length.
All opposing circumstances must be displaced.
So that peace can run its' course like
the meadows that are flowered laced.
Inside of every soul there lies a special place.
It has been there all along like a smile on a happy face.
The pace may be slow but it's thrilling
like a hole that has been aced.
The search is over it's the end of the race.
We no longer have to look because
in every heart there lies a special place.

133

"Take A Stand"

Of course there is cause for alarm.
Move out of the pathway from harm.
Don't dwell in the presence of pity.
Be hungry for knowledge to understand
that versatility is witty.
Wise men have the upper hand.
They search for wisdom so that they can take a stand.
For every course there's a reason
but it doesn't always explain, why?
We should never give up this is more reason to try.
Be an example to the kids it means a whole lot.
Try and think positive to give what you've got.
"Be responsible," that's a command.
Time is getting short, so take a stand.
Real men are needed to save our land.
Men of morality are in demand.
Do not neglect to be active in the role.
Responsible adults teach the correct way to reach the goal.
Be the leader of the band.
Do not build a house on sand.
Ears will hear music that is grand.
Righteousness is a solid foundation to build on and expand.
Wear it like a brand. Be a man and take a stand.

134

"Claim It"

Whatever the desire is from the heart claim it
to be yours. The words that we speak are pow-
erful enough to open closed doors.
If you want a wife then stake a claim. If you
need a husband then say his name. Negative
words can bring a person pain. Unlike posi-
tive words that can offer someone gain.
Work on speaking positive words bit by bit. There's
no pressure in being positive if we claim it.
If I want something then I must first believe that
it is mine. Just because I know that there's a sun
doesn't mean that everyday I can see the shine.
If I take medicine does it mean that my health
will be fine? I'll just claim that things will be
straight so that I can walk that line.
Life is great when we speak confidence in one word.
Love, it is not the result of what we heard.
It's an action or a verb. Kick the doubt to the curb.
If we want things to work then name it.
If you want it to be yours then claim it.

135

"Tasty"

Taste the goodness of the flavor.
It's a privilege a granted favor.
To acquire love in it's prime.
We have to be patient all in due time.
When things are as good as we desire.
Emotions ignite into flames like a two alarm fire.
The sounds of happiness is in the air.
Smiles and laughter are what lovers share.
The smell of your scent when I miss you I crave.
So all of my scenes of you I save.
You are beautiful on the outside and within.
That's the way that I see you again and again.
Making love doesn't have to be a physical touch.
Just knowing that I have your love is more than enough.
I've been chased, pinned down, cornered, and set free.
But none of those relationships
have been able to satisfy me.
I've put in my order for love
and got you right on time not hasty.
Our love is a well prepared dish, seasoned to be tasty.

136

"Yearning"

That day that I was called out of the darkness into the light.
The voice I heard said to me,
"Warrior prepare to fight."
I worried about my weapons but the voice said, use
your might.
I didn't understand what it meant so he told me.
"There is power in doing right."
I dropped to my knees the my stomach started churning.
Something inside me longed for the truth so I began yearning.
I was given a sword to practice and yield. So that I
could strike down his enemies on the battle field.
The more that I trained, I increased in my learn-
ing. The better things got the more I was yearning.
I am a soldier in an army that answers directly
to the King. That means divine intervention
so I don't worry anymore about anything.
I have been bought from the hands of death.
Upholding what's right until my last breath.
Our war cry is, "Victory,"
so tell the world the enemy is turning.

"Keep fighting prayer warriors
because the promises are on your heart,
that's why you're yearning."
"But for those that are not on our side
the lake of fire is burning.

137

"Get A Grip"

Why allow stress to win you over? Keep your
head held high while remaining sober.
A pig gets dirty when it takes a dip in the mud. But
wise men get a grip to grow into a flower from a bud.
Flattery has an effect, it can cause our hearts to do a back
flip. It can also result into pain if we don't get a grip.
Being cool is hip. So is getting a grip. Why frown and
drag your bottom lip? Life is good just take a sip.
A nip is a blast of cold. Get a grip means to hold.
If a hole in a boat can sink a ship. Then can
wrongful talk cause me to loose my grip?
Does an arrow have a sharp tip? All talk
is narrow without a tight grip.
Problem lash out like the force of a whip. To much
talk is like a constant drip. Keep control and zip your
lip. If it's out of control then you need to get a grip.

138

"Now and Then"

Things don't always go our way
and quite naturally the could.
Reflect back on some events the out come may
have been bad or it may have been good.
Every now and then things happen and we have no control.
Like getting pulled over by the highway patrol.
Not aware that the brake lights are out.
So we search for an answer to the question,
"What is this about."
Confusion does happen now and then, so what should we do?
Be ready for it now and also then too.
Stay alert like a light house on shore.
Who knows what is next or what will be
on the other side of the door.?
Now should be the time to get it right
because then might be to late.
If right is what we love then isn't wrong what we hate.
Now we have the truth, we also had it then.
Just like our past and our future we will encounter sin.
Now we have peace then we had strife.
Then we were lost now we've found life.

 ALAN ALSTON SR.

You are a winner who has been born to win.
Contend in faith and prop up your chin.
Be always ready to do right again and again.
We will always have time now but it may be to late then.

139

"Right Here, Right Now"

Right here, right now situations are about to change.
With endless possibilities who can measure the range?
Right here, right now respect my name.
Insults are futile because I know from where I came.
Right here, right now just mark my word.
I am about to take off and swore like a bird.
Right here, right now I will pray for us all.
Cushioning our steps so that none of us will fall.
Right here, right now I am wiser than when I was a youth.
Because all of my understanding is based upon the truth.
Right here, right now blessings over flow in my cup.
I have been granted favor because I refuse to give up.
Right here, right now I've been, ready to go.
Blow for blow, toe to toe.
Right here, right now there is no more
reasons to be stressed.
If we believe by faith then we have been blessed.
Right here, right now I am going to be the man.
I will use all of my authority
and my confidence because I can.
I'll thank God, so to my knees I bow.
My prayers will be, answered right here right now.

  Alan Alston Sr.

140

"Be Mindful To Take Heed"

Identify with these words they are not to be taken lightly.
Doing what we ought to means
that our performance is done rightly.
Be attentive my sisters and brothers.
If someone needs help then we should
lend a hand to others.
Obey the instructions of your father and your mother.
If the old way didn't work then try another.
Problems try and overcome us like a stampede.
They're evadable when we are mindful to take heed.
"How are we to be mindful to take heed?
By obedience that has been agreed.
It is by choice, yes it is indeed.
Discipline us also something that we need.
If we are trained well then we have the capabilities to lead.
We are blessed when we do a good deed.
Be mindful to take heed! A farmer plants a seed.
A flower can be choked by a weed.
Our minds we need to feed.
From knowledge that we read.

For the good of all people I will intercede.
It is for their innocence that I plead.
A body without blood will not bleed.
Be wise, be mindful to take heed.

141

"Will"

"Lets' suppose for one minute
that life is based upon good and bad luck.
Most of us will agree that life can truly suck.
If a problem comes at us then we should duck.
We should also watch our steps
before we are ankle deep in some muck.
We have a lot of concerns that we would like to voice.
But first we have to learn how to exercise our choice.
People face their problems based on how they feel.
Isn't the capacity by which we decide to do
or not to do something called our will?
Luck doesn't determine why the outcome
ends up a certain way.
Circumstances serve a purpose in our lives everyday.
The outcome can be voluntary by what we say.
If it is our will then we can choose, "yea or nay."
When we stay positive we surround
ourselves with good will.
Negative talk is the individuals' fault
resulting in bad pains that are real.

Focus on the decisions that determine a better way of life.
A person can will peace which will eliminate strife.
Peace means to be calm or to be still.
It's a decision that we all have, if it is our will.

142

"Faith Mends Broken Vases"

Life is filled with many ups and downs.
Problems are like people, they both populate our towns.
Temporary joy can come from the tricks of a clown.
Everlasting life is a gift that comes with a crown.
Live in joy with the life that you've been dealt
with even if it's not four aces.
A homerun can bring in four runs,
when there is loaded bases.
Outcomes may vary in different cases.
Just pick up the pieces of your broken vases.
Grace and Mercy will see us through.
But to believe in them, it is all up to you.
There's no need to wonder if you can make it.
Just believe that you can even if you have to fake it.
Even when we pretend, we stimulate a positive claim.
Go right ahead and take your aim.
Our lives are some times broken
like the vases that fall to the floor.
Maybe it's our eyes that need to be open like
the exclusionary places with restricted doors.

If we put a smile upon our sad faces.
It will bring hope in many cases.
Those without Christ are like broken vases.
That can't hold it together or win any races.
There are people that have him
because he has left them traces.
Giving away blessings others can see
in our lives that interlaces.

143

"Friend Or Foe"

There are two kinds of people in this world,
those that are with you or those that are against you.
Simply just watch what you say or do.
If you can feel the wind blow
the you can tell if someone is a friend or foe.
It'll be the way that they act that will help you to know.
Do your friends mostly tell you "no?"
Constantly trying to keep your self esteem low.
I suggest that you go.
Get them out of your life, that's not a friend that's a foe.
If you're trying to do right then stay strong.
A friend will guide you right but a foe will stir you wrong.
Even a wolf will wear sheep clothing so that it can eat.
And a fly will mimic a spider just to avoid defeat.
Everyone we hang with isn't always for the good.
Some people are around us
just to get as much as they could.
The friend is always someone that will help us grow.
The enemy is the foe that causes us woe.
So stay on guard, alert and on your toes.
Because knowledge is there to help us bless
our friends and wisdom will expose our foes.

144

"My Part"

I have been authorized to do my part.
Our abilities to perform come directly from the heart.
Life is not a game it is a commitment to maintain.
My job is to lead, correct, serve and provide.
I have a position to instruct, teach and to guide.
Just like a mule is destine to pull a cart.
It's my destiny to do my part.
Listen and understand the direction of my effort to assure.
I have the responsibility
to encourage the poor and the pure.
We all will endure hardships whether young or old.
Turn to the truth because that is what lightens our load.
My deeds to intercede can be marked upon a chart.
Because my dedication to love plays a major part.
My part is to praise others when they try and do their best.
Welcoming everyone into my life as if an honored guest.
Showing favoritism to none but being a friend to all.
Paying attention to my kids footsteps
so that none of them will fall.
My time hear on earth is where it will end
and eternity is the start.
Let it be known all over the world I will do, my part.

145

"Job"

The rules are as followed ever since
God had established that man should work a job.
Adam worked in the garden
and named Gods' creatures which in itself is a job.
The positions we are given
complements our obedience to perform a job.
Performance is how well I am going to do on a job.
The terror of being broke is more than
enough to want a job.
So it's my job to understand that I need a job.
Questioning authority is not my job.
The right prospective defends my job.
It gives me insurance that I will have a job.
Rightful and positive thinking are examples of acts
and deeds that we should perform on a job. Excuses,
there is none when you need a job.
Everyone is required to work if they are able to get a job.
Poverty teaches us a lesson,
being rich isn't a blessing unless
you are creating your neighbor a job.
Follow these guide lines and act justly on the job.

Keep notice of the negative
then reverse the attitude to move forward.
Take every opportunity presented before you for success.
Given to you freely is a calculated plan
done publicly for private profit.
This is why we have the thought for today.
"Get a job."

146

"Practice Will Tell"

No matter how well we try to perform,
without practice we wouldn't know our full potential.
Having personal experience is experimental.
The trails that we face won't be
as worse as finding out that there is hell.
Training to live right speaks for itself
because practicing what we've been taught, will tell.
Career criminals spend their lives in an cell.
If amused by deceit a habit will swell.
A valley is also called a dell.
A low tract of land between two hills echoes a yell.
We frequently fail but practice will tell.
Make it a custom not to bail.
Why betray yourself and then end up with remorse?
Doing as we should guarantees
that we're walking the right course.
If you bridle a horse then it is under the riders control.
Directions shouldn't be made by force
but our actions should be under patrol.
A persons conscience is the internal knowledge
of right and wrong.

Making a conscious decision
to be effective we have to be strong.
Someone with a moral sense will do well.
Because they have learned what's been taught,
and if so practice will tell.

147

"All Is Well"

Difficulties occur so that strength in our faith may increase.
Always act accordingly and do everything out of peace.
Peace my friend and I've said this out of love.
May my blessings descend upon you like a dove.
I'll give away my love so that joy will prevail.
Giving all praise to my God, I hail.
Who is the head and not the tail?
If you know then all is well.
We can be poisoned by a rusty nail.
Even placed behind bars locked away in jail.
We're also subject to fail.
But forgiveness is for our avail.
It's so we won't end up in hell.
But in Heaven is where all is well.
A train runs along a rail.
A boat can move forward by a sail.
Everything gets done by an action or force.
To get to the root of a problem we must find the source.
Just sound the alarm or ring the bell.
Spite of the trails all is well.

A broken heart will wail.
The release of love will secure or bail.
Anything other than the truth is a tale.
Salvation isn't on sale.
There's no fee when it's free so it makes me glad to tell.
That there is a Christ and through him all is well.

148

"However"

If it takes forever then I will make sure that
I'm worthy to love you.
There's no question of, who?
It'll be the one that has always been on my side.
True love I can not hide.
Isn't love forever?
Whatever it takes, however.
In every kind of way.
Even in the words that I say.
I can't contain all of the thoughts that I have planned.
So too love, I'll stretch out my hand.
Nevertheless the things that I intend to do
will be measured by not degree.
That means that I am yours if you'd agree.
I'm only one person but still.
Every time you need me, I will.
However I come receive me if you need love for life.
Just imagine us husband and wife.
Even though I might leave first when I die.
I want you to smile not cry.

Until then I am here loving you and I'm not done yet.
It's been good ever since that day we met.
With you I feel no pressure so I'm willing to do whatever.
Regardless of what it is, for you, however.

149

"Wisecrack"

Hee hee, hah hah and quack quack.
It's not funny if someone falls flat on their back.
Give them a hand and dust them off showing concern.
You'll never know when it'll be your turn.
Shame can hurt like a smack, so don't be a wise crack.
Laughter is a form of joy and it is said that ignorance is bliss.
How can there be happiness in this?
It's sadness if your uninformed or uneducated.
It's foolishness if this is debated.
Why try to be mister and miss know it all or silly and sillier?
We could wind up in the cold
where it gets chilly and chillier.
Everyone should be respected there definitely is a lack.
You'll find yourself alone if you are a wisecrack.
Sarcasm is ironic when one thing is
expressed and it means the opposite.
Like someone telling you that their sorry
after you've deliberately been hit.
All jokes aside, I'm not trying to rattle anyone's cage.
Maturity comes at an expected age.

There is a time for comedy and a time and place to play.
Life should be taken seriously every single day.
So whether you are young or old,
Jill or Jack deal with the facts.
It's stupid to be a wisecrack.

150

"Rest"

There are things of this world that may cause us grief.
It's going to be that way, so is there relief?
It is yours upon your request.
Pray for peace and you'll receive rest.
If we quit worrying then anxiety will cease for the duration.
Keep working on yourself so problem cause a cessation.
The experience is a journey or a quest.
It is well worth it to receive some rest.
For the rest of my life I'm going to enjoy
my zest for what is right.
To cease an action can mean to stop a fight.
I've been invited to be a guest.
Now I can kick up my feet to get some rest.
Just lay out your problems, give them away,
don't keep them in.
They're not yours to keep,
if you've been freed from sin.
If we want something bad enough
then we should choose to do our best.
If I do my part then who's going to do the rest?

To be supported is to rest under and bear.
So that our assistance comes from the one that really cares.
Under the protection of Jesus is where I'll build my nest.
That is where my help comes from
so that's where I'll find rest.

151

"What About It?"

What about the two of us taking a trip far away?
What about you laying back and I'll massage you everyday?
What about it?
It's a strong possibility that there'll be stormy weather.
Well steady as we go through whatever.
Passion and commitment, seasoned with loving you.
The fire inside me burns for what I am about to do.
To you my love I'll reach out my hand to hold on to yours.
Your inner beauty is sweet
so that fragrance lingers from your pores.
What about me being your servant
and taking care of your needs?
What about all of my pleads?
What about it?
There will be evenings after evening
prepared just for your liking.
Oh boy, wouldn't that be striking.
So care free are my needs just
as long as there is an us.

One on One isn't that a plus?
What about, if you would agree?
What about it?
This is the main question that I would like you to answer.
If it's yes then I'll be yours forever,
even your private dancer.

152

"Visualize"

As we allow our minds to perceive
that two can combine like the strongest of potions.
Observing your every move I gain the notion.
My love stirs up your emotions.
Like rubbing you down with your favorite lotion.
Our future will be a new discovery ready to unfold.
Look into my heart as I come to you bold.
For the one that I marry for her there'll be platinum or gold.
Forever ready I'll be so that it will never grow old.
Receive my selection to choose the way that it's going to be.
As I visualize there will be only you that I see.
Your smile is enticing it tells me
that you are ready to accept my love.
All I have to offer is a sizeable amount
of tenderness that will take flight like a dove.
Allowing our sensuality to connect there
must be an understanding that's direct.
Together we will systemize.
Becoming one we will glorify.
I said, I'll be yours this I can't deny.
Now that I realize.
We can have the one that we visualize.
You and I have won because together, we are the prize.

153

"Reverse"

Just one minute, back it up,
the other direction is the way to go.
For some time now things have been predictable.
Pitiful. Is that so?
Wisdom can be interwoven in a verse.
Death rides in a hearse.
This is why I compel those who necessitate
the need to reverse.
Making my appeal I coerce.
If the truth is no longer necessary then the world is cursed.
Immorality is commonly nursed.
It is unlike direction that is pursed.
It's a collectable prize presented for the reversed.
Do not walk backwards but yet turn and to another way.
A new way of thinking can brighten up anyone's day.
A decision of change should ultimately come first.
Being disciplined by obedience comes
showers of blessings from Heaven that will burst.
Just stretch out your cup
so that it may be filled up quenching the thirst.

I will do what is best because
I no longer want to be the worst.
The opposite way is the reverse.
It can only get better, can it get any worse.

154

"God Does Apply"

Where does my help come from when I am able to get by?
Who wipes away my tears when I cry?
How will it feel when I die?
Hell is where non-believers fry.
I do believe so with the wings of an eagle I will fly.
In these things God does apply.
Who can teach a man to be a nice guy?
I'll just hold my head held high.
It is important to be truthful and not lie.
"Me oh my," God does apply.
He is sweeter than an apple pie.
He created seeds for food and one of them is rye.
I am confident in who I believe in
so that I am far from shy.
His existence I can not deny.
Through out my life God does apply.
Me and my Lord together forming a bond or a tie.
This is the reason that I testify.
At least until the day I die, I will try.
He rescued me from trouble and opened up my eyes,
that's why.
My God does apply.

155

"Mold"

From the bones in my body to the blood in my veins.
In the end only a shell remains.
Since the beginning life was fashioned to unfold.
The creator of all things made a man to be the first mold.
Everyone is different but a pattern stays the same.
We are in the image of Jesus whether whole or lame.
Adam was showy like a poppy.
So we should enjoy being a copy.
A facsimile of perfection.
Who we are going to be is cast under Gods' direction.
Inside a mothers womb the baby takes on it's form.
The same pattern is called the norm
It's not seasonal like a storm.
Individual gifts we are granted to perform.
A standard human we would think
should have all body parts.
Regardless of what we are missing,
God still molds our hearts.
Rejoice in the celebration and strike up the band.
Everyone's destiny has been planned.

By the manner of which we are kept safe by grace.
We are going to meet out creator face to face.
All who repent will walk along streets of gold.
If this is your hope then guard your soul.

156

"Justified"

Through faith Christians have been justified.
For on the cross it was Jesus that was crucified.
It was done for the remission of sin.
That which we are not supposed to do over again.
All have fell short of God's glory
because of sin but are justified by grace.
We are born into sin in the first place.
All sin is excusable until death after that there is none.
Only then is when our defense is done.
Throughout our lives we treat ourselves unfairly.
Asking for God's help, rarely.
Everyone can find forgiveness through Jesus.
This form of kindness will appease us.
Just like babies we are pacified.
When our needs are actually being supplied.
Christ is glorified.
If we believe then we are justified.
When we are justified by faith
we have peace with God which is a gift.
Granting us jay on a twenty four hour shift.

If we choose to do right then our decision is just.
If we want eternal life then repentance is a must.
Because there is judgment everyone will be tried.
Vindication can not be denied
when there is justice noting who is justified.

157

"Mercy"

Please hold back your wrath from me, Oh LORD.
Allow your spirit to keep me in accord.
At times I feel as if I don't deserve to be called your son.
Even though I understand that no one is perfect,
meaning none.
I come to you with humility
because it is you who put the breath into my lungs.
You also defend me when liars speak
false with their tongue.
You are always willing to forgive when I am sincere.
It is you, whom I fear.
Spare your servant from my own wrong doing.
Evil lurks around me, it is my righteousness that it's pursuing.
Have pity on me when I choose to do my will.
It's merely a compromise like, "lets make a deal."
I am only human so I'll pray for strength to endure.
It is solely by your spirit that I am sure.
Your mercy is the cure.
It allows my intentions to be pure.
Be patient because I want to do exactly
as you would have me do.

Obeying only you.
Don't restrain your blessings from my life.
Without them there's only strife.
Please do not curse me but anoint my head.
If you take away your mercy then I might as well be dead.

158

"Liberty"

"Give me liberty or give me, what?
Death isn't that like taking a shot to the gut?
If my freedom is being attacked then I must prepare for battle.
I refuse to be pinned down or branded like cattle.
There are eyes observing my every move, every day.
But safe passage has been granted
to me so that I can be on my way.
Privileged to go where ever I please.
I am privileged not to sin
and not to be stricken with disease.
Since we are free does it gives us a right to sin?
Of course not, so we should practice on not doing
bad things over and over again.
I would rather die because death is like a door.
Once I cross over I won't have to suffer anymore.
Disengaged from the oppressor and his tricks that deceived.
I'll stay immune because of Christ whom I received.
I'll stay thankful for liberty because my freedom is a must.
Authorized by God with license to be just.

159

"If I, Will You"

In life relationships last a life time when two agree.
Just be optimistic the you will see.
One plus one is you and me. You and I are we.
If I choose you to love, will you choose me?
If I didn't know how you felt, will you help me to see?
There are a lot of things that will not work if there isn't two.
A house is not a home when there is me and not a you.
If I give it my all then will you do the same?
If I offered to take your hand, will you accept my name?
Who can say how far we can go?
It will be forever if I have the say so.
If I make a mistake, will you forgive me first?
Will you give me drink if I have a thirst?
Will you be mine if I pass the test?
If I were your one and only, will you be my best?
There are endless possibilities for two to make it great.
I can't tell what it will be but it'll be worth the wait.
I've often wondered with who but I never knew.
If I said I do, will you?

160

"Utilized"

It is always the advantage to follow what is right.
The benefit comes from having a positive insight.
Given the proper resources any potential can be maximized.
Anything that is useful should be utilized.
Being familiarized with the instructions
of life we gain support.
A rationalized strategy will protect the fort.
Minimize any negativity so that wrong can't have it's way.
To stabilize a situation some believers pray.
We can observe the trouble but can't visualize what's the cause.
It's the aid of a stronger force that can neutralize or pause.
The general idea is to seek help everyday.
So to generalize wise advice there must be a common way.
Only then it is itemized. Taking note if it is personalized.
We seek counsel so that problems are sanitized.
Only critics criticize.
The proper aid should be scrutinized.
Is the bible hypothesized?
Only if we battle against sin then it should be utilized.

# 161

"Watch For The Rain"

It is said that, "When it rains it pours." Of course.
When the clouds gather overhead they make people wonder.
I will intend to be like those clouds
that you see high in the sky,
that brings the thunder.
I will strike with the force of a lighting bolt.
Exemplifying power that will put a lump in your throat.
No joke, so don't choke.
Never stand in the open, there might be regret.
Run for cover because you will get wet.
I am coming through and my efforts wont be in vain.
You'll know who I am, so watch for the rain.
Knocking on your window pane.
Stimulating my audience brain.
I will intensify my wind to break the chain.
Uprooting the wickedness that brings the pain.
What I'll take away will benefit in gain.
So that the senders glory will leave a stain.
The message that I have is very plain.
Take heed to the signs and watch for the rain.

162

"Legendary"

Here's the truth to consider.
For my efforts I will deliver.
I intend to be some one who knows that life is grand.
The righteous will inherit the land.
Just like impressions in the sand.
We all are people who hold
their destiny in their own hand.
Legends have been passed down since earlier times.
Now it's the twenty first century
and that means that one day some one will tell mine.
I will not stop to produce one hundred fold.
What will dull my shine,
when my heart gleams more than gold.
Yes, there are legends but most of them are old.
So now I am going to be a living inscription
that has to be told.
For good intentions and personal reasons it is very necessary.
Until then, through the end, I will be legendary.

163

"For A Cause"

Decisions, don't they apply to us all?
We will either stall or scale the wall.
Pause for a cause.
Applause for the best of yall and to rest of yall,
try not to fall.
Push to the front of the line.
Those in the rear will see your shine.
Monitor your time, you'll get no where if you wine.
Surprised by the depth well it gets much deeper.
Are you the stronger or the weaker?
You will be one or the other.
Uh, uh I did not stutter.
When it's cold the body shutters.
If it gets to hot to hold don't switch to the other.
Out of my mouth I utter,
wisdom says, "use pot holders," my brother.
If able then milk this thought like utters.
Stay clean not cluttered.
It's creamy like butter.
It's your decision, nah it's your call.
Just give it your all, for a cause.

164

"Appreciation"

The meaning is to value
and from value there is precise signification.
To present importance is the initial application.
There should be appreciation for life
even under a dreadful situation.
Appreciation for someone
or some thing we declare to be worthy,
giving distinct notification.
If we value something then we estimate
that it'll be ours for the duration.
It specifies great worth or prices a desired quotation.
Appreciation and love have a connected relation.
Intertwined one without the other there isn't liberation.
There's a genuine appreciation for peace grants
love offering a number of constellations.
Appreciation for a mate is conformation.
When commitment is true there is verification.
Together forever verifies, no grounds for separation.
Held high in honor there is edification.
Devoting our life to a person shows dedication.
Marriage is the motivation.
Affiliation constitutes appreciation.

165

"Mark My Word"

Trouble doesn't last always.
Everything works out through calculated days.
Instruct a child by teaching them the truth.
By doing this, it will save a youth.
There are many good ideas to teach.
If we are to make a difference
then we should practice what we preach.
Mark my word.
The law is for those that commit wrongful acts.
If we obey the laws then we are exempt
from punishment and that's the facts.
Information is power expressed in words.
"Doing wrong is for the birds!"
A saying doesn't always mean what it said.
We can choose one thing but do the opposite instead.
Mark my word.
There is peace for those that believe it exists.
The opposite is hardship for those that resist.
Mark my word.
Weeping endures only for a night.
Joy comes in the morning, a delight.

Mark my word.
Opposing the truth is false, "now that's absurd!"
Upholding what is good is always right so now you've heard.
The truth we should seek, just mark my word.

166

"Is Love Expected?"

When we come together there's a bond of un-separation.
Together is the classification.
Forever if it'll last the duration.
Beautiful it'll be if it meets a required expectation.
Idea's of a perfect mate are collected.
This may be why the wrong one is often selected.
In our hearts we truly want the best.
But in our lives we often neglect or reject the rest.
None of us are perfect, meaning that everyone has a flaw.
If you are someone that obeys
then why would you be with someone that breaks the law?
We expect to be loved but we hardly ever wait.
Rushing into relationships with someone that hates.
Only to find our lives effected.
Stricken by love that the other rejected.
Afflicted like a disease the heart can
be broken or neglected.
The ones that work together are the ones protected.
The choice should be commitment
if a relationship is elected.

Love has a proper way of working
out things when it is honestly directed.
Yes, I would say that love is expected.
Because if our feelings are respected
then by waiting we will be affected.

167

"Could It Be?"

Something beautiful happens when two are in love,
would you agree?
A natural course of action uniting you and me.
Like the birds and the bee's or the flowers and the trees.
Love is free, which goes for he or she.
It's a sight to see.
Happiness and glee.
I'm speaking of now thinking of us and we.
Could it be?
Commitment shouldn't be taken lightly.
When we agree a bond is formed tightly.
We will be loving one another nightly.
Making our days shine brightly.
Respecting each other politely.
Our decisions will be make rightly.
Could it be?
Deeper than the sea.
Sweeter than tea.
It very well may be.
Oh, yes indeed.
We are, all that we need.

Could it be true that I don't have to wait anymore?
I've found the center of our hearts and love is the core.
True love flourishes like a flower by a stream.
Was that you that I wanted in my dream?
Could it be?
Are you the really the one for me?

168

"It's All Good"

Today is no different from the rest.
Why not treat each day like it's the best.
A response toward an unpopular
situation is what we call getting mad.
Just like a practical joker, " you've been had."
Don't play yourself, it's all good, "not bad."
Playing it cool comes in handy.
We might find ourselves in a lifestyle sweet as candy.
Cling to an outlook that states,
no matter what everything will be okay.
Pestilence has no power over the spirit
of joy if we cherish love everyday.
Being attached to the wonders of belief makes life great.
This I've learned to appreciate.
Be thankful in the way that we should.
Living grateful makes it all good.
Living is not at all crappy.
When people are uncertain they are not happy.
Live for the promises of life like I live for mine.
It's up to individuals to get theirs
because one day things will be fine.
Join in to share my joy if you would?
It's like shouting O' boy when it's all good.

169

"Direction"

Looking out of a window we can see
a lot of people going to and fro.
Coming or going only those individuals know.
Down the highways across the by ways
on the sidewalks or off the curb.
The direction we take should be an action
of what we need to do or a verb.
No one forces us to choose one way or the other.
When our minds have been made up
it is slightly different or another.
Live to do what is right is in demand, not a demand.
Go and do right gives a command.
It points toward the act of doing what is right.
The failure to comply warrants a fight.
There are courses of action like stop, no and don't.
But the only choices we have are, will I or won't?
There are only two directions, either, or.
One is open and the other is a closed door.
When we follow directions they instruct us on what to do.
If we accept them or not it's all up to you.
Guidance can lead a person toward peace and joy.

It has been the same direction that I took as a boy.
Which gives an attitude a course straight for correction.
Those that want a brighter day will
choose the right direction.

170

"Time Won't Wait"

The degree of speed or to be classed
in a certain order is the rate.
That's the way we choose our living while life
is getting shorter but time won't wait.
Perhaps we've lost time trying to meet the right mate.
Or could it be that we didn't set out fresh bait.
Nevertheless time won't wait.
Experience teaches because now we understand
that things don't always go as we plan.
But two shipwrecked hearts
will be rescued if they agree that they can.
Given the exact.
We comprehend a known fact.
This is true, "time wont wait."
Leaving no room for debate.
It has been proven time and time again.
Things might not come soon but patience brings a grin.
Now that's a win.
Consider your state.
Under the conditions that we're dealt
with we still can't change fate.

What's going to happen will happen and time won't wait.
Who is able to set the date?
It's the one that allows only goodness to enter the gate.
Welcoming love and rejecting hate.
So if we understood, what is,
then our thinking won't be late.
Get what's yours while you can because, time won't wait?

171

"Ownership"

Why is it that when we don't want something anymore,
we decide that it's our as soon as some one else wants it?
Homerun, now that's a hit.
Is it selfishness or ownership?
Either way here's a tip.
Everything that we get we should work for it.
The less effort involved the more that it will be a little bit.
Just like most relationships.
If it doesn't flow then we end up only with drips.
When there's a piece cut from a diamond the fragment
still has a price of it's own.
If some one gives a piece of there
heart then treat it like a loan.
It should be paid back with interest to the donor.
To hold on to a promise makes you the owner.
When two join together in interests there is partnership
me for you and you for me there is ownership.
If two acquaintances posses love
then new friends are not hard to find.
A situation can bring two together
but in a relationship two combine.

When a gift is given the motive should be clear.
What is mine can't be taken away because I hold it dear.
The truth is in most relationships,
we need to get a grip.
Without the commitment
of the other there isn't ownership.

172

"Sunshine"

It may have rained out doors
but you have made my day bright.
The time we spent together was such a sweet delight.
Everything was going so smooth
I felt like the time was right.
If it had been dark outside
I wouldn't have noticed the night.
Maybe I could sum it up in just one line.
Back in the day I knew that the sun would shine.
Your smile brightens up the room clearing a path just for fun.
Let's play chase the rain away and you can be the sun.
Friends we have always been and to this day
things are still the same.
I've asked you to come on by and you politely came.
We are all grown up now and sunshine is your name.
Since no one can hold you down
doesn't that make you fair game?
You are beautiful, radiant and you can make it hot.
I will always be patient if you promise to unthaw my spot.
Curiosity was there the moment
you walked through the door.

Impressed by the way you shine has me
curious of what's in store.
Juicy fruit grows on a vine.
Intoxicating like wine.
When the two of us combine.
Everything is fine. Sunshine.

173

"Take Control"

If I am humble with good intentions
then why do I stumble and don't pay attention.
I've realized that I can't do it all.
Is there some one to hold me up so that I won't fall.
I am on a mission or you can say that I'm on a roll.
I do get tired of driving but I have to reach my goal.
Some days are harder that the others but I've learned to cope.
Spite of my weaknesses I will exercise some hope.
I'm bothered all of the time right after I've done wrong.
It doesn't make me proud yet I know where I belong.
I'm hard pressed on ever side even though I'm moving along.
I may have disobeyed but I'll sill sing the victory song.
I won't give up trying because I'm not dead yet.
So if I die trying there won't be any regret.
I've realized my mistakes while praying
that I become whole.
To my knees I'll drop feeling sorry and my spirits low.
Looking forward as I approach another
bridge blocked by a pole.
Will I be able to cross over if some one pays the toll.

Instructed by he keeper of the bridge
that I can pass and go.
He saw that I was for real
when I allowed Jesus to take control.

174

"Longing"

Love is clearly visible when it is natural
and doesn't indicate doubt.
Just allow nature to take it's course
then a man will show a woman what his love is all about.
Earnestly desiring the uniqueness of his spouse.
Upholding all of the necessary duties
to safeguard their house.
We may not all look the same
but some of us still think with their brain.
Using intense logic and reasons that are obvious
so that his love will maintain.
Such a desire only comes
when he has been chosen by his equal.
The woman that this man longs for must
exhibit a quality that has no sequel.
The art of her character enlightens other people.
Then that man will acquire
an appetite destine for the steeple.
Wishful searches have failed
and maybe others could have been.
The longing never cease when his love starts to begin.

Isn't love unconditional
and doesn't that mean it never stops giving.
A heart felt desire that distinguishes
love for two that is worth living.
A man only desires a heart
that is connected to his belonging.
Until then there will still be men that are longing.

175

"Wounded But Not Dead"

Over the centuries right up until present day
many have been knocked down but not counted out.
Hearing the loud cries of pain as wounded soldiers shout.
Still alive is what I'm talking about.
Breathing in faith and not living with doubt.
Survivors of any drama should rejoice instead.
Because we are only wounded but not yet dead.
Prisons hold the freedoms of men
and women inmates and prisoners of war.
Caged, is that what rehabilitation stands for?
Kids are being shot yet some of them are still amongst us.
Some one just wanted a seat so she sat
at the front of the bus.
A dream that is on the move is still a plus.
It's not over that's why there's still a fuss.
Miracles right before our eyes so that our faith is fed.
We all are wounded but not quite dead.
Crash victims, the crippled and the hearing impaired
can live a life.
Even some of those that are diseased still believe
they can be freed from strife.

Everyday people like mothers and fathers even
I will one day mourn.
Beaten and battered, tattered and torn
because of sin a savior was born.
Be part of the body because Christ is the head.
Jesus did rise wounded but not dead.

176

"Re-evaluate"

Most of us would like to do things over again,
maybe start over with a clean slate.
Since our minds are occupied
by this subject we can relate.
Life will get much better at a faster rate.
When we re-evaluate.
If we aren't going anywhere
then we should rethink our position.
I wanted things to get better so change
sparked some ambition.
Don't leave a mess the way you found it.
We should reconsider not to go around it.
If we re-evaluate our motives then right
and wrong will show up real clear.
There's nothing wrong with knowing
the truth so why is it what some of us fear?
To value carefully means to evaluate.
Or to ascertain the amount of,
to make certain like finding out a exact date.
Make a stand the recalculate.
Making our life exact again we compliment our fate.

It's a blessing to fix the mind on not sinning again.
To re-consider the endless possibilities all we do is win.
The thought should be taken seriously
but it is often under debate.
Change should occur, it normally leaves us in a better state.
It is to never to late to re-evaluate.
As long as we live why wait for insurance
that is straight to the gate.

177

"At last"

Finally, the moment I've been waiting for.
I heard your voice then my heart yearned for more.
Years have passed by and I've only been
able to see you at a glance.
It's not to often in life when love
can be given a second chance.
I had you in my grip but I let you go.
No, not again because back then I didn't know.
I am a man of love but there's no one to share that with.
I can love you if your the one,
not the second, third, fourth, or fifth.
We haven't saw one another lately
but I can hear the love in our voices.
If I had it may way then you would be with me,
my one and only, no more choices.
I've been in relationships but true love I didn't see.
Now it comes natural so I want you to be with me.
Like the ocean my love is vast.
It'll make you happy
because I can love you like you my last.

I haven't had these feeling before not even in my past.
I just know what I want so that's why
I'm giving you my feeling fast.
I my not get this opportunity again
but I know that if we love one another it'll be a blast.
I've always wanted a wife maybe I'll have one at last.

178

"Have A Seat"

Pull up a chair my friend
and take a load off of those weary shoulders.
Why do you still carry around those old problems
that are a heavy as boulders?
Times are rough and I know that you're beat.
Just calm down, have a seat.
What's been bothering you lately?
What you need is rest and I mean, greatly!
There will always be problems
but we don't have to live in defeat.
We have to go through them it is impossible to cheat.
Oh, you say that your troubles are at it's peak.
Well why don't you take some wise advice and seek?
When you search for peace, you will gain a treat.
Because when you find it then you can have a seat.
There's a narrow road and many broad streets.
The many are bitter days but the narrow is so sweet.
I wonder why do people continue
to live their lives as if a repeat?
Life the worm they end up out of the dirt and into the heat.

Dried up like jerky meat.
There's a need for something healthy like a loaf of wheat.
Since we are friends can I tell you something neat?
When I asked Christ to enter my life
he a carried my load, so that I could have a seat.

179

"Sexy"

The quality of your character moves
me like the feel of your touch.
I can hear your body language which tells me so much.
It says that you are elegant and tender.
This attracts me to the opposite gender.
Your posture is upright just like you insight.
Now that makes you sexy and that's alright.
It's all about you, "Yeah that's right."
Like the sway of those hips in your jeans that fit tight.
You're not to flashy but you shine just enough.
You are a classic like a diamond in the rough.
That makes you quality and tough.
You got that right stuff.
Your words appeal to my intellect when you talk.
My eyes are fixed on your moves when you walk.
You have those sexy kissable lips.
I can't leave out those enticing switch-able hips.
Your eyes flicker of subtle passion telling me that it's okay.
Your attitude is refreshing like the showers of April and May.
You know exactly what to do and what to say.
Oh, and you stir up my emotions by the way.
Exciting me like a child ready to play.
Sexy, what more can I say.

180

"Someday"

There are a lot of things that will occur one day, for sure.
For depression, peace is the cure.
Struggles, we must endure.
There will be success when our motives are pure.
Troubles come in a vast array.
But through it all they will end someday.
Our hearts can sing of joy filled
with the beauty of a blue jay.
Expressing our outspoken testimony with no delay.
Someday we can lay all of our burdens down.
Unleashing a smile from a frown.
Have an open mind because the conscience leads the way.
Illuminative blessing are scattered throughout
our lives as a display.
We are granted mercy every morning awaken by the suns' ray.
If we are stripped of mercy then the body will see decay.
Remember what I say. Love, you may.
Be eager to pray.
Things will be okay.
Sacrifice has been the price of pay.

One life for all sins he lay.
The creator fashioned us like clay.
His kingdom is on it's way
and we will be with him, someday.

181

"Wanted Expression"

Give me a minute or two of your time for the sake of love.
Understand that my intentions are only to receive
what is mine before I shove.
My true feelings are an expression of affection in a song.
Out of forgiveness I ask you to forget
about the times that I've been wrong.
Our conversation makes it okay
and that's just one of my suggestions.
Get ready because her are some more wanted expressions.
Showing affection toward
a broken heart can produce healing.
So let's think about how important dedication
and commitment are toward your lover
and what they are feeling.
Two can eliminate the pressures by protecting
one another with sincere motives of trust.
Connecting their hearts over riding infatuations and lust.
Why not before we start something
pray first for a little intercession?
We'll never know if we could have avoided
a lot of unwanted expressions.

Broke apart will be the out come
leaving a heart without protection.
Cheers to the one that I join with, for we will have direction.
We will be aware of what we have
only to be focused on perfection.
Wrapped in love until death do us part
filling all of her wanted expressions.

182

"I've Always Been This Way"

I've been this way ever sine I was a child.
Growing up in the projects
without direction just running wild.
I've made some bad decisions in life but I'll never quit.
I've played some dirty games
and even made my enemies sit.
I didn't recognize my potential until a man died by my hand.
Bitter and lost, needing help, I just kept sinking in sand.
My heart had compassion but angry is where I stood.
Why is it all bad for the people in my neighborhood?
My mother struggled but she taught me
the better things in life.
Everyday outside my eyes saw pain and strife.
I could recognize love but giving it back did cease.
Please forgive me all I wanted was to find peace.
Give a child bad and that is what they will likely be.
Teach them the ways of God then one day they may see.
My eyes are now open and I stand as a man.
Prepared for battle to fight evil as much as I can.
Advancing in the ranks praising the Lord everyday.
Ever since I could remember, I've always been this way.

183

"Think First"

Before we give a response we should consider
the words that roll off our tongue.
Wise selections display maturity
between the adult and the young.
A blabber mouth is only good for one thing.
A lot of perverse talk and sin is what that will bring.
Put a guard on your mouth
because our words can leave us cursed.
Regret might be the outcome if we don't think first.
Judge for yourself what are the right words to say.
If you give the wrong response then
you might have to pay.
It's very important not to use flattering words for per-
sonal gain.
And don't believe a deceitful tongue
because flattery is extra ordinarily plain.
It is obvious that we should consider the words
that we listen to and the one's that we speak.
Two many words can be disturbing like a drip or a leak.
Nothing is quite like falling off of a shelf.
If we speak of a lie then we testify against our self.

Imagine being caught and forgetting
the lie that was rehearsed.
Judgment will fall on the guilty and their folly at it's worst.
So before you say a word remember this verse.
Blessed are the wise that always think first.

184

"Fruitful Expectation"

In life we look forward to a lot of good.
Like wishful thinking of what could.
One could say that fruitful expectation is productive hope.
Believing in faith without rejections of "nope!"
Pleasingly satisfied our hearts raised in celebration.
Like waiting to receive your mate is a fruitful expectation.
Liberation for those in bondage requires optimism.
Which gives us the tendency to take a more
hopeful view unlike pessimism.
For those of us that look forward to a positive outlook.
They may find abundant joy like
catching a large fish on a small hook.
To look forward to is not in vain.
Only when the situation is inconsistent
and it doesn't maintain.
Disappointment leaves us in pain.
But when there is fulfillment
of what we expect then joy is the gain.
Understand this, our expectations
don't always come through producing edification.
Morals build up discernment for conformation.

Which verifies a conscience of purification.
Look for the good to come out of every situation.
Positive reinforcements leave such a power of sensation.
It excites the interest desired when we receive
the reward from a fruitful expectation.

185

"I Care"

If we are someone that shows concern
then we should feel fortunate and that's the case.
Leaving us standing on a foundational base.
This condition I am very aware.
So through out my life I will be a man that cares.
I care about all things.
From the Most High God to the smallest birds that sing.
From the Ohio River to every brook and spring.
Happiness is what I will bring.
The truth came to me one day
to light my way and set me on a course.
But before I was able to leave
I had to be cleansed of all bitterness and remorse.
If we think with a renewed mind then we will receive
some impressionable thoughts to share.
This is one of the reasons that I will always, be able to care.
I care about all people all of the time.
Those that can restrain their flesh
and the one that does the dirtiest crime.
We should all be people that show compassion
on everything living but these kind of people are very rare.

It was the pain that Christ suffered
for me that made me willing to prepare.
I asked for forgiveness and he did, now that was fair.
One day where He is I will get there.
I challenged my faith to a double dare.
He believes there is good in all things,
that's the reason why, "I care."

186

"Irresistibly Attractive"

Just like a magnet, two hearts can draw toward one another.
Attracted for whatever reason latched to the other.
Held by commitment love is the glue.
It's a demand for unity expected to be true.
Intertwining spirits together in life.
Joined in union God blesses the husband and wife.
When two desire a common bond.
There will be an attraction
to grow together above and beyond.
Devoted time insures delight.
Dedicated to please in always alright.
Unbreakable ties are hard to unlatch.
Undeniable love will insist to attach.
It's irresistible attraction rather we're ready or not.
A plan to unite gathered by a plot.
Fasten your seat belts for a relationship ride.
Catch a wave to surf the high tide.
So value what you have this means to have pride.
What God has joined together let no one divide.
Unlike a drug and far from a disease.

Love is unconditional, it's objective is to please.
Just honor your mate and keep respect presently active.
Then and only then will we find
them irresistibly attractive.

187

"Nerves of Steel"

Let's suppose for one minute
or just maybe my words are for real.
Being someone that is eager to act displays zeal.
In the mist of trouble be ready to deal.
Or refer the outcome for an appeal.
No sweat just use your will.
It's sometimes better not to act on what we feel.
Approach any matter with caution, relax and chill.
It's not good to be shaky so have nerves of steel.
Even now and until.
If you climbed the mountain then you can hike up a hill.
If we don't work then we can't expect a meal.
If something gets infected then time will help it heal.
On a wise mans tongue he places a seal.
For when he opens his mouth
you can find choice morsels like veal.
Seek the truth and you will have your fill.
The account of life is due so pay your bill.
Why struggle with trouble?
"Peace be still."

Those that know God are the ones the devil will try to kill.
But they are protected 365 days year round like a wheel.
Allowing grace to keep us
producing faith with nerves of steel.

188

"Spirits Talk"

Clearly unseen but the conversations
of spirits are heard primarily inside.
Not from the haunting of a ghost
but from person to person on an internal ride.
A smile gives a greeting without saying a word.
Isn't this talk without uttering to be heard.
Speech isn't our only form
to communicate an idea or a notion.
A friendly look from some one on the beach could imply,
"Would you help me with my sun tan lotion?
Polite and angry spirits can be recognized.
By the character that we display our attitudes are verbalized.
A stuttering explanation could indicate untruth.
A stable childhood testifies in behalf of our youth.
If a person wears a frown this may mean
that their spirits are down.
If some one walks along the highway
then they could need a ride toward the nearest town.
Conversations without uttering a word are very real.
By the way when we act or react
tells others the way that feel.

People can have good ideas and thoughts
that are detected by the look on their face.
An umpire can use a hand signal that declares a persons place.
We don't have to make excuses when others see us at fault.
Our actions give a report of the way spirits talk.

189

"Troubles Won't Last"

Preoccupied by the thought of the storms
that we have to go through.
Many hours even days without a single clue.
When will it all be over is a good question
that deserves an answer.
Everyone has trouble but be sure to endure
there might not be a cure like cancer.
Do the righteous suffer like the bad?
Of course, but in the end it
will be the righteous that are glad.
When prayer and praise goes up,
blessings come down.
Those that have faith will be bearers of a crown.
Dressed by God wearing a white gown.
Called up to dwell in a Holy town.
There will be streets of gold transparent like glass.
A new city of its' own class.
Out of the darkness into the light.
Press on to persevere and fight a good fight.
Focus on the Lord and never lose sight.
I'll testify on his behalf because he has made it right.

I've had heartache and pain,
been in terrible storms and light rain.
Nothing stays the same.
So to you my request is plain.
Just call out one name.
Jesus... said that it will pass.
He promised that our troubles won't last.

190

"Good News"

Extra, Extra read all about it.
There's reason to rejoice and no need to doubt it.
Hope for the best and pray for even better.
Joy comes to the heart when we receive
a long awaited letter.
Consider my words, "Why sing the blues?"
Christ is our savior, he paid all of our dues.
Once I couldn't perceive.
Now I truly believe.
I use to be worried with strife.
But now I live a new life.
All because of change.
Now that's nothing strange.
I haven't always been this way.
Until one day I had to pray.
God, please come my way.
I'm in trouble and I have to pay.
Facing me was confinement locked up in a cell.
As bad as I felt my soul was going to hell.
I asked the Lord to forgive me and now all is well.

Trouble still tries to find me
but the good news I have to tell.
The good new is the hook and my testimony is the bait.
If you don't think that you have faith
the ask for it and wait.
All across the world there are believers that fill the pews.
They know like I now because they too have good news.

191

"Concentration"

A primary focus should be under consideration.
Avoiding destructive forces requires concentration.
Direct all energies to a distinct object.
Deal with the matter and the content of the subject.
Objectives can be defined as purpose having intentions.
Obligating our thoughts far beyond the surface
of the mind forms petitions.
The mind will invite fresh new thoughts of penetration.
But the one I solicit to you is the one called concentration.
Be a solicitor for direction.
Because those that concentrate in life place
themselves under intentional protection.
If there's discrete thinking then it's not apprehensive.
When distinctly focused our mistakes
won't be that expensive.
Concentrating on the way
that we live should be of great concern.
Thinking about objectives will help all of us discern.
For the sake of improvement focus on being a discerner.
A clear-sighted observer has the eagerness to be a learner.
For the thoughts that I profess zeal is the motivation.
Enthusiasm is preferred for concentration.

192

"I Insist"

There's a direction that leads us to a potential height.
Respond to the unlimited possibilities without a fight.
Disregard fear, I know exactly how it feels to be afraid.
It does get exciting when we partake into a quest to serenade.
If love ever approaches you are not to resist.
Take it to heart, I insist.
The many problems in life we try and juggle.
But the most influential ones we tend to struggle.
Hold on to the good things in this life, I insist.
Without them there's no assist.
You do expect a little help at no cost.
The value of it is to be found and not lost.
Shackles and chains no longer bind our feet and wrist.
I can now live in the freedom the way that I insist.
Weaknesses often hinder our potential to grow.
So confront any issue that may drag you low.
Reverse all negativity into a positive twist.
Grab wisdom with a tight fist.
Summon some help for an assist.
Then you will find that everything
you need is in your mist.

Remember this, people will love themselves
and money, they will be boastful, proud, abusive,
disobedient, ungrateful, unholy, without love, unforgiving,
slanderous, without self control, brutal, not lovers of good,
treacherous, rash, conceited, lovers of pleasure rather
than lovers of God, and having some godliness
but denying its' Power,
so do not be apart of this list, I insist.

193

"Directional Thinking"

Stop, look and listen there are other
directional commands that I didn't mention.
Like beware, prepare, always share and never compare.
Some courses guide us toward grief.
While others are not the way we would
like but they do allow us relief.
Use your head in determining the pathways that you take.
We won't always choose the right ones'
but it's okay to make a mistake.
Why worry about our food
and clothing like the animals, their not concerned.
If we work then money can be earned.
We study knowledge so that wisdom is learned.
Even the desire of a loved one can be yearned.
Direct our thinking means to order
our thoughts in a certain manner.
Instruct yourself to be examined closely
using the mind as a scanner.
All of the ifs', ands', and buts'
really don't amount to much.
Maybes' are also categorized as such.

Indecisive reasoning isn't absolute.
A conclusive response deserves a salute.
So therefore remember that the truth is what life is all about.
Uncertainly is meaningless which raises some doubt.
A person without direction is constantly sinking.
And the one's that have learned
their lessons use directional thinking.

194

"Intended for Good"

Talented gifts and special abilities should be well respected.
If they're not utilized then their purpose is neglected.
All things are intended to work for the good
of those that love the Lord.
The bible teaches many wonderful precepts
that penetrates like a doubled-edged sword.
The meaning of this analogy means
that it can cut on both sides.
Slicing through ignorance and cutting through pride.
Wisdom is intended, along with humility if we abide.
Noted by many believers that use it as a guide.
Study to show that you have been approved.
Confirmation gives authorization to be at peace in trouble,
unshaken or unmoved.
Intended for good states that it's designed for usefulness.
That which is designed without
importance is meaningless.
When we share our abilities with others
that find them amazing to do.
We're often praised for our goodness
to receive what we are entitled to.

Could death be intended for good?
The answer is, "Yes," it could.
If all my life I lived in strife then suddenly a loved one died.
It could be the straw that broke the camels'
back to move me inside.
Life and death are intended for good
no matter how we perceive it.
Just like the Bible is, regardless of who believes it.

195

"Staring Out My Window"

As I stare in a glare wondering what is out there.
For me, myself and I, will prepare.
Looking beyond my direction I can see perfection.
Felt by a spiritual connection.
Believing for myself I just want to share what has been bare.
Just a look out the window
to see for myself because I care.
Thanks to the beautiful days along with sunrays.
Bless what the rains may wash away,
on my knees to the Lord I pray.
This confirms that my heart still humbles low.
Walking through the cornfields of life reaping what I sow.
The natural order comes about due to a plan.
By nature I am a mammal but dominion came to a man.
Complete with the right to choose.
My will has to be the same will as my spirit or I will loose.
It's fortunate that I've decided just to be
patient as a seed that will one day grow.
Organizing my priorities putting all of my ducks in a row.
Even the birds are being fed, how do I know?
Because I observe staring out of life's window.

196

"Do You Understand?"

This question has only two answers,
either we do or we don't.
Some will try, while others won't.
Life is not that hard when we live it to win.
Times do get difficult if we flirt with sin.
Problems can cause obstruction like an enormous wall.
But the enlightenment of understanding
is to see you through it all.
None of us have all of the answers
but at least attempt to do the math.
Of course we should concern ourselves
with this matter before we end up off the path.
If we learn the ways of how we could be tricked.
Then we should recognize that we might not be licked.
Discernment is to understand
how a situation really seems.
Our stronghold is the truth that can penetrate all schemes.
The decisions that we make are the reasons
things are the way that they are.
Oops to late now I'm left to live with a scar.
To perform in our right mind we use intellect.

Right should be our thinking causing
our actions to be direct.
All I've asked was, "Do you understand?"
Because intelligent folk are well informed
they've followed the instructions and listed to the command.

197

"Simple"

Let's reflect on a simple thought of truth for our sake.
There are multiple options in life
but only one of them is not a mistake.
This is not an opinion formed by a mere man.
It is a collective agreement shared
by those that build according to a plan.
If we don't have an outline then I suggest a positive outlook.
Life is a prospect by which some of us are hooked.
Comforted by a simple motive to insure safety zones.
Constantly on a search for precious metals or stones.
The treasure that I speak of comes from the heart.
Like the passion for wisdom and knowledge
it's a great place to start.
For me, I will constantly question my own motives
to steer away from strange places.
Take poker for instance a royal flush
can triumph over four aces.
As an absolute direction has insurance against sad faces.
By this I know that I am going
to fill the void of those empty spaces.

While certain affiliations can grant us the upper hand.
Others are unsafe to build on
like building a house on the sand.
Place your index finger on the place
between the forehead and the ear,
which is called the temple.
This gesture symbolizes that we're thinking
complex thoughts that are not, simple.

198

"Judgmental"

In our vocabulary there lie words that can cause litigation.
Many other words judge and lawsuits
are quite common amongst our nations.
Who can judge amongst our people,
the millions of humans that believe?
Is anyone, capable of actually telling
the other how to perceive?
I think not.
So now lets kill the drama to see what we've really got.
Individuals can gauge for themselves what they've done.
Having good sense isn't that common
but it's second to none.
We a have our own opinion or belief.
But of our own actions, you are your own chief.
If we are slightly inclined to use good judgment
then the notion to be positive has a direct effect.
Now that's a call for improvement, what do we expect.
Good sense isn't common and common sense isn't that good.
There are different varieties of trees
so there are different values of wood.
Give situations and people the benefit of the doubt.

There could be slight possibility
that we might not know what it's really about.
Time will tell but will we be able
to proceed with that first thought?
Perception is discernment, which is to understand
the difference in being at fault.
What I am saying, is be careful if we point
the finger it could be detrimental.
The good that we see as bad
is an opinion which is judgmental.

199

"The Wrong Way and the Right Way"

Let's look at the title, there's either, or.
No in between but understand what they are for.
The right way is to go at a gradual pace.
But the wrong way will have traps
to knock you flat on your face.
How can we lose if we do what is right?
I've learned for myself that kindness ends a fight.
It takes strength to turn the other cheek.
I then realized that I was far from being weak.
If I would have continued on then I would have been wrong.
Hurting myself, all along.
Giving others the benefit of the doubt
can put the mind and heart at ease.
But bitterness will kill the both
of them like a deadly disease.
For a better life going the wrong way has to cease.
The right way is the only other option
if we want constant peace.

Be wise in your thinking, wouldn't you rather think smart?
Sure, we all would, so do your own part.
Just because you've chose not to go the way that loser go,
doesn't make you less.
It actually says that you are better and that, is so.
There's a way that seems right
but blessing won't come every day.
That's why we as people get all that we deserve
trying to do it our own way.

200

"Initial Response"

At first I pretended not to acknowledge
that I was attracted to someone quite like you.
But for natural reasons I knew what I had to do.
I knew that I had to let nothing get in my way.
Only if you had initiated the conversation
then I would've had a lot to say.
If you really want true love to start
then show me the way into your heart.
It begins with the initial response and ends with,
"Dinner and wine."
You with me I know that everything will be fine.
My needs are to meet yours.
Be a little more curious then you will see
that love even flows through my pores.
See, at first my initial response was to just leave
the situation alone.
But love kept calling me, so I answered the phone.
Hello, I answered, is it me that you'll put some faith into.
Just believe that it will happen, tailor-made only to fit you.
Our walk together will be stride for stride.
The initial response will be to let the Lord be our guide.
Then we can go for and wide, in love we can confide.
I will be the Groom and you can be the Bride.

"Love Never Ends"

As I know love it is the truth.
Which has always been, ever since my youth.
Love is now and also later.
One who loves is never a hater.
Love gives accommodations meaning that it lends.
Love furnishes in a supply that never ends.
If we delight ourselves with someone or something,
tell me how is this strange.
Only because society uses the term lightly
they we helped it to change.
People say they love then take it back
as if they've made a mistake.
"What's the meaning of this?"
All that it means is that lover was fake.
What is unconditional isn't false.
It is absolutely indefinite, fond attachment isn't a loss.
This is again regarded with affection to maintain.
So to love someone who doesn't love
us is why we feel the pain.
Love is acted out by what we do.
It is intended to benefit two.

At the crack of dawn through the twilight it extends.
It carries along with it a message of reality that it sends.
It is unbroken eagerness to please that is capable to mend.
This is the truth that Jesus gave for you
because his love never ends.

202

"Trying to Reach You"

One day out riding along the avenue. I saw you.
My intentions were only to speak
but that was kind of hard to do.
A man of my standard seeks a quality friend.
You are lovely on the outside
but is that quality the same within?
If you knew what I know then you could see as I see.
But of course I'm going to represent myself
because there's only one of me.
Fun, loving, spirit filled and free.
If you're that same way then
what a grand friendship this could be.
Occupied we are but I wonder what could I do?
Our other relationships have passed
and may be our old partners didn't have a clue.
It takes two, true?
I'm not a fast pace runner because patience
says wait on someone but I wonder, who?
If you knew me then you would know
how well I would treat you.
Others know what kind of man that I am but you don't,
that's why I'm trying to reach you.

203

"Just For You"

It seems so very simple to mention all
of the things that I say I can do.
The most important of all things
to know is that I can, love you.
Just like you like it, service with a smile.
Everything that I intend to do will be worth your while.
I think that I know what you have been missing.
Unconditional love with hugging and kissing.
I know someone just for you. "Are you curious?"
Me that's who.
Would you mind starting over fresh with someone new.
Just for you, I'll be your cuddle toy like Winnie the Pooh.
If you need me by your side I'll stick by like glue.
I will massage you feet.
Even tell you that I think you are sweet.
I have to always do my part because we can be a team.
I know how I feel, this is real, not a dream.
You and I equal, two.
We mix well like vegetables in the stew.
I see love as a perfect view.
Sun shining days with clear skies that are blue.
Do you know what I'm getting at or do you have a clue?
If I give you me then that means my love is just for you.

204

"Hail to the King"

Here Ye, Here Ye, as the spirit calls.
Hail to the one that is here to save us
and tear down Satan's walls.
The creator of all things great or small.
Salvation is available for one and all.
I offer Him praise and the worship of His glory,
I must sing.
Let the world bow down, "Hail to the King."
You can have anything that you desire
but a tenth is all that, you said bring.
Your mercy and justice are forever, "Hail to the King."
Trouble has always followed me but I'm protected, under-
neath your wing. Your are Christ our Savior,
"Hail to the King."
You serenade those you love,
unconditionally for life, is your thing.
The guardian for the poor and the widow,
"Hail to the King."
In you I can boast and to you, I do cling.
You promised not to leave us or forsake us,
"Hail to the King."

You took David into battle with Goliath and gave him
victory, with a sling.
It was you that guided the stone,
"Hail to the King."
I am thankful that you are in control and Supreme,
over everything.
You died on the cross for all,
"Hail to the King."

205

"Complex"

Completing a task takes obedience.
Oddly as it my seem, it is so hard to stay on target.
Approaching different obstacles, angles and measures.
Complexity can hold some hidden treasures.
Deep as one extends their own horizons
and broadens their mental capabilities
the can induce pleasures and pain.
That person has developed an complex way of living.
Right or wrong can be compromised,
bringing ones' true nature into existence.
Self-sufficiency takes place,
if irritated it can develop into desires.
Unquenchable thirst.
Understanding our potential to rebel,
simply constitutes disregard for morality.
Questioning motives enables u to have
a way toward a higher degree of excellence.
Making life, complex!
This should direct a challenge toward an individual
seeking the fruit of a place not yet inhabited by them.
Seek and ye shall find.

Curiosity will drive a person to examine all the facts.
Curiosity makes life complex
with matters that are emphasized by feelings held back.
So aim for your direction.
There will be times of trouble
but for your labor there is reward.
Search for the answers and there will be
a place for mistakes.
Make every effort to understand
that doing things our own way
brings consequences if not handled with care.
Watch yourself and grow.
You will be in the right place
for knowing that life is for a reason.
Which is more reason to open up to the truth,
of what is and has always been!